The Taylforths are a big, c... talented and warm-hearted ... 29, was cast in the BBC's new... role as Kathy Beale rapidly fulfilled the producer's prediction that it would make her a 'household name' ('Like Domestos, you mean?' muttered her father). But she soon learned that while it was one thing to be stopped in the street by admiring autograph-hunters, or by people confusing her with her TV persona and offering her advice (or even ticking her off!), it was quite another to be interviewed by an apparently sympathetic journalist only to see her words distorted in the next day's headlines.

Eventually, in 1994, after enduring almost a decade of such treatment by the press, Gillian and her family courageously took on the police, the media and the most expensive lawyers in the land when they decided that the gossip and the lies had gone too far. The outcome of the much publicised trial nearly destroyed them all, and Gillian became the focus of almost continuous media attention.

Kathy and Me is Gillian Taylforth's autobiography. She describes with wit and exuberance her childhood, her teenage years, her first forays into acting and her current lifestyle, recounting scores of anecdotes about home, family and experiences with other members of the *EastEnders* cast, both on and off the set. It is a moving and often funny story of a woman the nation has hugged to its heart – and almost crushed in the process.

This new paperback edition contains an additional extra section, bringing Gillian's story right up to date.

...ose-knit London family whose ...second daughter, at the age of ... the soap opera EastEnders, Gillian's

KATHY AND ME

GILLIAN TAYLFORTH

with

ANDREW CROFTS

BLOOMSBURY

First published in Great Britain in 1995

This paperback edition first published 1996

Bloomsbury Publishing Plc, 38 Soho Square, London W1V 5DF

PICTURE SOURCES

The publishers have made every effort to contact all copyright holders.
Any who have for any reason not been contacted are invited to write to
the publishers so that a full acknowledgement may be made in subsequent
editions of this work

A CIP catalogue record for this book is
available from the British Library

ISBN 0 7475 2645-1

10 9 8 7 6 5 4 3 2 1

Typeset by Hewer Text Composition Services, Edinburgh
Printed in Great Britain by Cox & Wyman Limited, Reading

To Jessica and to
the memory of my dad

Acknowledgements

First and foremost I'd like to thank my mum, sisters and brother for their love and tireless support through good times and bad, and also the rest of my relatives and friends for their unflinching loyalty. Special thanks go, of course, to Geoff and to his mum, dad and family for all their faith and encouragement. Thanks, too, to all the cast and crew of *EastEnders*, past and present, who've made the first ten years such fun; and many heartfelt thanks to the thousands of people who wrote in or stopped me in the street during and after the dark days of the trial to offer their good wishes and solidarity. Thank you to my agent, Sara Randall, and particular thanks to Andrew Crofts who has skilfully put on paper what I could only express in spoken words. Special thanks also go to my literary agent, Robert Kirby, who got my book off the ground, and to my editor, Penny Phillips, who has been kind, supportive and wonderfully professional.

Contents

1	The Family	1
2	Still at Home	13
3	The Acting Bug	23
4	Leaving Home	31
5	On Safari	43
6	The Big Break	53
7	Getting into the Papers	69
8	The Rape Scene	81
9	Nick	93
10	Geoff	109
11	Dad Dies	121
12	Carrying On	129
13	A Day at the Races	145
14	The Nightmare Begins	151
15	More Stories in the Press	157
16	Fighting Back	169
17	The Video	179
18	The Verdict	193
19	Into the 'Boneyard of Damaged Reputations'	201
20	Battered But Not Broken	217
21	A New Year and a New Start	229
22	So, That's What Happened Next!	233

1

The Family

There were dozens of us, brothers, sisters, uncles, aunts and cousins, all living off Upper Street in Islington, mostly in four neighbouring blocks of private association flats: Victor Cazelet House, Salisbury House, Robinson Court and St Mary's. It was all my mum's family, the Borers, and we were right at the centre of it. St Mary's Church was next door to the flats and the church clock used to sound every hour. Visitors could never imagine how we could sleep, but you don't notice that sort of thing when you live there. It was the church where we had all the family christenings and weddings and funerals.

Islington was a wonderful place to be brought up, right in the heart of London. At the bottom of our path you could catch a bus to anywhere you wanted, getting to the West End with all its shops and cinemas, clubs and restaurants within a few minutes. We were a few minutes' walk from Camden Passage, where all the antique dealers set up their businesses and the crowds come to browse and haggle. The King's Head Theatre and the Angel were just round the corner. Gradually we have seen the area become fashionable with trendy media people moving into the streets all around, doing up the houses and bringing a lot of money to local businesses. Nowadays Islington is full of fashionable restaurants, but it hasn't lost the character which I remember as a child and most of the same families are still living in the flats.

The atmosphere of the area came from Chapel Market, which was going six days a week, with stalls selling everything from jellied eels to shoes, winkles to overcoats, crockery to flowers. We knew all the stallholders and they knew us. We still know most of them. When it comes close to Christmas they keep the stalls open and go on trading until midnight; I can remember the thrill of going up there with Mum and Dad after tea, all wrapped up against the chill of the winter nights. The whole market was lit up and the stalls were covered with Christmas lights and tinsel. Victor Hollister, the jellied-eel man, always claims he was my sister Debbie's first toyboy, when she was nine and he was eight. He went on to get married and have two daughters and then had a vasectomy. When my sisters and I all started to have babies at the same time, old Victor got broody, seeing us wheeling the pushchairs around on Saturday mornings, so he decided to have the operation reversed. Now he has a little son and he's thrilled to pieces with him.

Mum and Dad had five children and I am the second eldest. Debbie is a couple of years older than me and Kim a couple of years younger. Then there is a bit of a gap – Ronnie was born when I was about seven and Janice the year after. Mum and Dad were mad about old films and their stars, particularly the musicals, so Debbie was named after Deborah Kerr, Kim after Kim Novak and me after the choreographer Gillian Lynne. Ronnie was named after Dad, who always said his name came from Ronald Colman. By the time Janice came along I think they must have run out of star names. Things could have been worse – one of us might have been called Ginger, or Cyd.

They never meant to have so many of us – Mum had only planned on having one, but birth control was a bit hit and miss in those days, and there wasn't any telly to watch in the evenings. So there we all were and we couldn't have been happier. Mum and Dad were the most wonderful parents.

They lived with my nan and grandad in their flat for a while before we got our own place. Dad always referred to his in-laws as 'Mr and Mrs B'. I used to love listening to Nan and Grandad talking about their memories from the beginning of the century. They both worked at the Post Office and we used to go to the most brilliant Post Office parties.

My aunts, uncles and cousins also had flats around us. We all used to go away together in the summer to holiday camps down on the coast. We were always entering one another for events without saying anything, so we never knew what we were doing until we heard our names called out over the tannoys. One year my cousin and I went in for a fancy-dress contest as Andy Capp and Flo from the *Daily Mirror* cartoon. I shoved towels up the front of my shirt and down the back of my knickers to get that shape of hers – and we won!

We used to go on a coach and you could bet that Mum and Dad would fall out while we were getting ready, because Mum would always insist on cleaning the windows and making all the beds so that we would come back to a nice house. This was on top of getting us ready, packing the cases and all the rest. She would probably have been up till three the night before ironing all the clothes we needed to take with us, then in the morning Dad would get up, shave and dress himself while she dealt with us, did breakfast and prepared a packed lunch. Dad would then be ready to go and would want to know why she was so long getting herself ready. By that stage she was usually not in the mood to be wound up and used to give him an earful.

Dad had very strict ideas on what jobs the woman of the house should do and the man should not, like all the washing, cooking, ironing, child rearing, housework and the rest. Poor

Mum never had anything like a washing machine – she was always scrubbing away with a rubbing board at the sink, wringing the sodden clothes out with a mangle and hanging them out to dry on one of those racks you pull up to the ceiling, the sort of thing people cover in dried flowers these days. There were always nappies boiling on the stove in a big pot. Now I've got a child of my own I can't imagine how she managed without all the conveniences we take for granted.

Dad was very intelligent and had won a scholarship to Highbury Grove, a top grammar school at the time. He worked in the print department at the Rubber Stamp Company and I don't remember him ever missing a day's work. Mum, whose name was Margaret – although Dad only called her that when he was cross, usually calling her Marge like everyone else – was always at home with us until we were safely off at school. Then she went back to cleaning. When we were little Dad used to bring home work from the Rubber Stamp Company, like labels to be addressed. Mum used to do that and sometimes I would help her, to earn myself a few bob.

When I was born they were still living with my nan. Then they moved to rooms of their own. There was no running water in the rooms; if Mum wanted a tap she had to go down a flight of stairs to a tiny sink on the landing. The one toilet for the whole block was at the bottom of five flights of stairs, so when Mum fell pregnant with Kim, Dad bought us a bucket with a lid so that Debbie and I didn't have to go downstairs every time we needed a pee. He would empty the bucket for us when he got home from work.

When Kim was born, a man Grandad was working with found us some rooms in a basement. One of the rooms was condemned because of the damp, but at least Mum and Dad had their own bedroom and Debbie and I had our own room. We used to use the condemned room as a playroom and we had some brilliant family parties in it. We then moved to a top-floor flat, where we had our own bathroom, which was luxury. My main memory of that home was Bonfire Night one year, when Dad wouldn't let us out because of the danger. He was home, having his tea between his day job at the printing firm and his night work behind the bar in a local pub, and he had promised to take us up on the roof to watch what was going on outside before he went out again. While we waited for him to finish his dinner we all went to the sitting-room window to look out. A rocket came up and smashed through the window, a shard of glass went into Debbie's arm, the blackened remains of the rocket went straight into Kim's eye and I got burned as well. Kim had to be rushed down to Moorfields Eye Hospital, to have her eye popped out and cleaned.

We were living on the top floor of Robinson Court, in a three-bedroom flat, when we discovered that Kimmie, who was five by then, had developed kidney trouble. The doctors told us that we had to get a ground-floor flat before she could come out of hospital, because the stairs would be too much for her. Mum, who had had Ronnie and was pregnant with Janice, went to the Housing Association and by luck they had a four-bedroom flat available on the ground floor in Salisbury House. We moved in and Mum and Dad lived there for nineteen years, until after we had all finally left home. The flat had a long, dark hallway with all the rooms leading off it, and a tiny kitchen. I loved it there because as the others left to get married I finally got my own room. It was a bit damp, but Dad did his best to treat it. We had some wonderful times there. There was a little garden where we kept all sorts of things, like my tortoises and the damaged pigeons which I had found and brought home to nurse back to health. One of these pigeons I hid in my room without telling anyone while I went out to school. Mum heard some noises in the room, opened the door and the pigeon exploded in her face with a great crashing of wings and scattered feathers, sending her screaming down the hallway with the poor bird flapping around her.

I was at church one day and heard some miaowing coming from under the floorboards. I went out the back to look for a way underneath. Finding a gap I could crawl into, I waited for my eyes to become accustomed to the darkness and there, cowering in a dusty corner, was a frightened-looking little kitten, whom I immediately christened Tiddles. I managed to get her out and took her home to Mum, who told me in no uncertain terms to take her away. I wasn't about to abandon poor Tiddles again, so I took her to the vet, who cleaned up her eyes and said I would have to feed her from a dropper and wipe her little bottom for her once an hour. 'I could take her for you,' he said, 'but I would probably have to put her down.'

'Oh no,' I said, 'I'll look after her.' So I went home and told Mum that the vet had said I had to look after Tiddles. She wasn't keen, but she gradually softened as she watched the poor little thing fighting for life. We had to take shifts through the night looking after this sad little creature as it lay on a blanket in a biscuit tin. In the early hours of the morning, when it was Dad's turn with the dropper and cotton wool, Tiddles raised her hackles at him and keeled over dead. I cried my eyes out when he told me the next morning and asked what he had done with the little furry body. He showed me where he had buried it in the garden and I made a lolly-stick cross, stuck it in as a headstone and prayed over it, racked with grief. Years later Dad was reminiscing with me and a boyfriend, warning the young man that if he took me on his house would end up like Doctor Dolittle's, and he accidentally admitted that he'd thrown Tiddles' body in the bin that night, not buried it at all. I went mad at him.

Everyone loved Mum and Dad; in fact when I started going out with boys one of them didn't want to break up with me for fear of hurting them, never mind about me. Dad was always joking, doing old dance routines whenever the music came on. I think I was the one who was most like him with the jokes, always the one to get up and do his routines with him, the first to make fun of myself and to clown around. Often when there was a gathering of the family at weddings or after Christmas dinner Debbie, Kimmie and I used to put on shows for the rest of the family. We used to mime to records by people like the Jackson Five and the Four Tops, but our favourite number was 'Under the Apple Tree' by the Andrews Sisters. Kim used to use her skipping rope as a microphone and I made some keyboards out of the kitchen table, with Debbie on a guitar made from a tennis racket.

If we were stuck inside in bad weather we would dress up in Mum and Dad's clothes, putting on little plays to amuse ourselves. We dressed Ronnie up once with a scarf round his head, high-heeled shoes and a dress. Dad was always terrified Ronnie would grow up effeminate from being brought up with so many girls, so the sight of his only son clip-clopping into the front room in drag nearly drove him mad. He made us strip Ronnie down and promise never to do that again.

Mum and Dad loved watching musicals on television. I can remember at least once a week we all used to sit down in front of things like *Annie Get Your Gun* and *Calamity Jane*. If I could have been any of those stars, I think it would have been Doris Day in those western films. Anything with Fred Astaire, Ginger Rogers, Gene Kelly or Cyd Charisse in they adored and the rest of us were swept along by their enthusiasm. I always liked the romantic stories of boy meets girl, boy loses girl, boy gets girl again. My favourite was *Brigadoon*, about the little town that comes to life once a year – wonderful.

There was never much money about when we were young, but we had whatever we needed. Mum always knew where she could take us for things like school uniforms, where they would let her pay weekly. Each holidays she used to take out a Provident cheque, which was like a loan, and she could buy what we needed from the shops that took the cheques, paying the money back a little at a time. She always used to dress me, Debbie and Kim in exactly the same clothes until Debbie started to rebel. I remember one outfit particularly, with bright red flared coats and little bowlers that we used to call our 'Acker Bilk hats'. When we were little, Kimmie and I shared a double bed, but I kept shoving her out of the way because she wanted to cling to me. I pushed her out so often she started to cry and ended up sharing with Debbie, so I would have the room to myself for the rest of the night.

At school I was good at sports. I was athletics captain of my house and I swam for the school and won lots of medals. I got my school colours for gymnastics and I passed 'O' level English. I was in the Girls' Brigade as well, which meant that I had to go to church on Sundays. I really liked religious knowledge when I was at school – the Bible seemed to have such good stories in it. I still love church services, particularly candlelit ones. I always get a lovely warm feeling when I'm there and I feel so close to the other people. It's the same sort of feeling that I get at Christmas time, when everyone is really happy and friendly to one another. Mum says I'm too much of a romantic, always looking at the world through rose-coloured glasses, which is why I am so easily upset about things. I'm sure she's right, but I don't think I can change that now.

Kim and I became very involved in Sunday School, going there for years. Eventually I was asked if I would like to teach some of the younger children and I jumped at the chance. We used to talk about stories from the Bible and see how they resembled things that were happening now. We'd sing a few songs and do some drawings. We used to go to Wales for the Eisteddfod. Debbie and Kim both have wonderful singing voices and I could just get by when I was with them.

A bunch of us, including Debbie, a friend of hers called Lesley, a couple of other girls and me, used to put on plays for the people at the flats during the summer holidays. We would stage them in a corner outside St Mary's House, round by the sheds. We'd put up a curtain to change behind and have all the mums sitting outside in the audience. One year we did *The Pied Piper* and the next we did *Peter Pan*. We would go round to all the flats with a shopping basket, telling people we were going to be doing a play and asking if they would like to contribute anything. They used to give us sweets and biscuits. On the day of the performance people made us sandwiches which we could hand out in the interval. We made our own posters to advertise the performance and stuck them up around the flats. No one in the family ever imagined that Kim or I would actually become actresses. Debbie was the one Mum used to call Sarah Bernhardt. Once when she was very small Mum sent her to bed for being naughty and she reappeared in the front room a little later, completely silent and staring straight ahead of her, unflinching until she had Mum dancing around her, apologising for getting cross with her. Debbie went on being a drama queen and when she was older she joined the Islington Shakespeare Company at the Players' Theatre. In one school play she was a magician and had to join the Magic Circle, going to see Ali Bongo and swearing she would never tell anyone the secrets. I spent hours in her bedroom in the evening trying to work out how she did the tricks, but she never gave anything away. I was up for a part in that school play as well, either as a courtier or as the queen. I really wanted to be the queen because it would have meant having a nice costume and walking about the stage doing a stately dance, but another girl got the part because she had a bigger bust than me – I think I was still wearing a vest at the time. I was the tomboy of the family, more interested in climbing trees and messing about outside than anything serious or feminine. I suppose nothing much has changed – certainly not in the bust department, and I doubt if I'll ever be cast as a queen now!

I became more and more interested in performing as I got older. By the time I was a teenager I was taking piano lessons at the Angel and go-go dancing at the Dance Centre which had opened in Floral Street in Covent Garden. I used to have to dash from one class to the other and it got to the stage where I was so exhausted I collapsed. Dad put his foot down and said I had to give up one of them, so I decided to stop the piano – much to his annoyance. I wish now that I had kept it up, because I had been doing it for a year and I was beginning to get the hang of it; if I had just persevered a bit longer I would be able to play today, which would be great. But dancing won out. I loved it so much and still do. Whenever I'm at a disco I'm always out on the dance floor, more often than not on my own because I can't find anyone who has the stamina to keep up with me. Dancing really takes you out of yourself.

As a child I got a lot of sore throats, making my voice sound croaky and unnaturally deep for my age. Mum took me to the doctor and I ended up going to hospital for tests, swallowing mirrors, having samples taken and God knows what else. Eventually I went in for a stay of a few days and exploratory surgery. They found nothing, but suggested that I should see a speech therapist about the depth of my voice. The therapist did all sorts of tests.

'Well, Mrs Taylforth, I can't see anything wrong,' he said to Mum. 'Are you worried about it?'

'No,' she replied.

'Don't worry,' the therapist said to me. 'I think you've got a lovely sexy voice, you'll probably earn your mother millions with a voice like that.' I was relieved to hear that, but it was a bit embarrassing when I started going out with boys whose voices were still squeaky, or just breaking, while mine was already broken. Once I started acting Dad constantly referred to me as 'the female Arthur Mullard'. He used to tell people I 'walked like a navvy and talked like Lee Marvin'.

We all spoiled Ronnie and Janice, him because he was the only boy and her because she was our baby sister and she was so cute. While she was growing up Debbie, Kim and I all had Saturday jobs and we used to buy her whatever she wanted. While I was still at school I worked in a little chemist's shop in our road for an hour and a half after classes had finished and on Saturdays. Then I lied about my age to get a job up in Chapel Market in the shoe shop.

During one of my early days at the chemist's a man came in and asked for 'a packet of French letters'. Well, I had heard of Durex, but I didn't know they were known by any other names.

'French letters,' I repeated thoughtfully, 'right you are,' and I went over to the stationery section looking for something with an airmail sticker on it so that it could be sent to France. I couldn't see anything, so I went back to the customer, where he was waiting at the front of a growing queue.

'French letters, you said?' He nodded, obviously wanting the earth to open up and swallow him. 'Pam!' I shouted out to the back. 'Where's the French letters kept?' Pam came running through, but not as fast as the poor customer went running out of the shop. The Durex were kept in the top drawer and there was another man who used to come in regularly and ask for 'a packet of top drawer'. He always wore his full motor-biking kit, complete with helmet and visor. I'm sure he didn't even have a bike, it was just to cover his embarrassment. Another woman used to ask for 'a packet of soft centres'. I learned a lot.

2

Still at Home

Dad always wanted all of us to work in a bank because he thought that was a really secure job. 'You'll get a good mortgage for later on in life,' he told us. 'They'll help you out in all those ways.' But none of us was that keen.

I left school at sixteen and got my first proper job with the BBC, working as a clerk/secretary for the *Radio Times*. Debbie was working there as well and they said they couldn't have two sisters in the same department, so I had to go down into the basement to the picture library. I used to sort out all the pictures that were to go into the magazine. I stayed a year, but I didn't like being cut off without any windows. I used to have to run upstairs every half an hour just to see the daylight.

The BBC let me go to college on day-release to take further typing exams and after a year I moved on to a company that sold business machines. My job was to send the boys out to fix the machines. I was still a bit of a tomboy, never wearing make-up or anything like that, and it was my boss at my next job, with Allied Breweries, who suggested that it might be an idea to start wearing a bit of mascara now that I was eighteen.

The only time I had used make-up before was when I wanted to go out dancing with Debbie at the Tottenham Royal when I was fifteen. The Royal was a wonderful place, full of plastic palm trees, where I could dance myself into the

13

ground and then drink 'snowcaps', made of crushed ice with juice poured over it. Debbie had insisted that I should try to look older with a bit of mascara. I had complained at the thought of having to be bothered with such 'sissy stuff', but I had been keen enough to go to do as she suggested. I also bought a second-hand mohair suit off my friend Janet, which I wore over a little short-sleeved Ben Sherman shirt with a button-down collar. But the best bit of the outfit was a pair of black patent shoes with mirrored heels – I thought they were so smart. I must have looked all right because a nineteen-year-old bloke started taking an interest, but he had a lady tattooed on his arm, so I made him wear long sleeves when he came home to meet Dad.

Unfortunately, when I started wearing make-up for work I was always putting it on in a rush and I ended up scratching the cornea of my right eye. It never healed properly, so every so often the cornea tears again, leaving me with a swollen and painful eye.

It's amazing how many magazines and papers ask for beauty tips when they are interviewing actresses. I know practically nothing about make-up and beauty routines, and there are so many things I don't like about my face and body I could do a whole article just on them. I've got a body like a footballer and calf muscles you wouldn't believe. When I put on high heels they come out like bullets. I hate the way my ears stick out at the top and I've got this 'cow's lick' at the front of my hair which has always driven me mad, and of course there's my chest which is virtually concave. The list could go on for ever.

I was always keen on keeping fit, though, doing aerobics and going to the gym to work out with weights, and I have kept that up. Even though it can be an effort to get there, I always enjoy myself and I feel wonderful afterwards, much more alert and sharp. I played goal defence in a netball team for Allied Breweries. When I first went to work on *EastEnders* I found that I was constantly going to the chocolate machine to get something to eat during the waiting periods. I really started to put on weight and I could see that they were going to have to widen the doors of the Queen Vic just to get me in and out, so I started to eat more sensibly and take regular exercise.

Dad had always been very strict with us, although he was much more lenient with the youngest two when it came to their turn. It was like two separate sets of rules. The first three children had been brought up in the old-fashioned way – if we did anything wrong we were made to stay in for the week. By the time Janice was in her teens, parents couldn't get away with that sort of discipline any more.

I never wanted to rebel against my parents, not for more than a few minutes at a time anyway. Debbie and Kim left home long before I did. Debbie got married at twenty-one, and Kimmie went off to live with someone, but I stayed on. I loved being at home with Mum and Dad, and there was simply no reason for me to go. I didn't find any of their restrictions too bad. One night when I was about sixteen I went out to the pub with Debbie and some friends and Dad told me I had to be back by ten o'clock. Debbie wanted me to wait with her for a boy and it was about eleven by the time we all strolled home. Even in the dark and at a distance I recognised Dad's walk as he came to the top of the path. There was a boy walking quite innocently along with me, while Debbie and her bloke lagged a bit behind. Dad headed down the path towards us and I could tell I was in trouble. He came up to me and clipped me sharply round the ear.

'Get down here, young lady, you're in for the week!' He turned to the young man. 'Thank you very much, good night.'

I was so embarrassed when he did things like that, I called him all the names under the sun, under my breath. But even as I was staying in after getting home from school each day, I always knew they were doing it for my own good, trying to protect me. Now I've got my own little girl I appreciate even more the worry that you go through as a parent.

'You just don't realise what it's like for us when you are out,' Mum told me once when I was going on about it. 'We imagine you out there with your throat cut. When you don't get home by a certain time your dad gets so worked up that by the time you do turn up the only way he can release it is to give you a smack.'

He would never go to sleep until we were all in, and any sound like a scream outside the flat would have him bounding out to check it wasn't one of us. If we brought a boy home for a cup of coffee and Dad was supposed to have gone to bed, he would keep coming out of the bedroom and flushing the toilet to let us know that he was still around and we weren't to get up to anything. His favourite line if we arrived in late was always 'We'll talk about this in the morning!'

One evening, after a night out at a club, a friend of mine called Edward offered to walk me home. Edward is black and has the most beautiful, posh speaking voice. When we got to the front door he asked if he could just use the bathroom before going home. I showed him where it was in the darkened corridor and went into the sitting room to wait for him to finish, closing the door to give him a bit more privacy. Dad must have heard us coming in and decided to make one of his warning trips to the toilet. Just as he came out of the bedroom Edward came out of the bathroom and they came face to face in the dark. Both of them screamed and put their hands in the air as if someone had stuck guns in their backs. I came running out of the sitting room and found them, face to face, both shouting for help with their hands up. When we had managed to calm Dad down he couldn't stop talking. 'I put my hands up,' he said, 'and his went up. I thought he was my bleedin' shadow!' Edward couldn't stop laughing when I told him what Dad had said.

One night, soon after Debbie had started work, we heard a scream outside at about the time she was due home on a Saturday night. Dad was mucking about with one of Ronnie's toy guns and he ran outside without dropping it. A bloke had come out from behind a car and made Debbie jump. Dad came hurtling out of our flat, brandishing the gun. The bloke panicked and ran into a dead end, so Dad caught him and started laying into him with the barrel of Ronnie's gun. Mum was right behind and joined in; they were both shouting, 'You touch our daughter!' and he was protesting, 'I never touched her!'

'He didn't touch me, Dad,' Debbie joined in. 'I was just frightened he would.'

So Dad let the man go and didn't call the police. Much later Debbie admitted to us that the man had touched her, but she had been frightened of what Dad would do if he knew. This incident made Dad even more protective of Mum and us than before – he just wanted to keep us wrapped in cotton wool all the time. I think in many ways his protectiveness was harder on Mum than it was on us. He hated her to go out on her own to anything, even down to the pub. If she was at all late getting back she would get exactly the same sort of treatment as he gave us.

Another night when they were waiting for one or other of us to come home, Mum had already gone to the bedroom and put on her nightie. She had one leg out of her tights and was about to get the other out when someone screamed outside and they were off again, with Mum hanging on to the spare tight-leg as she galloped along behind Dad. This time it turned out to be a domestic dispute in another flat.

Our brother Ronnie has become just as protective of us all as Dad was, particularly of Janice. Once, when we were living in an upstairs flat, Janice's ex-boyfriend and another friend came to the door and started to give Janice a hard time, not realising that Ronnie was sitting in the front room, listening. After a while he stood up – and he is a very big lad – and walked out behind Janice. Without saying anything he came out on to the balcony, lifted them up, one in each hand, and held them over the parapet until they got the message.

After my various childhood pets, Dad had banned me from having any more because I always got too upset when they died. But we heard about some friends of ours who bred bull terriers and Jack Russells. Unfortunately, one of the Jack Russells had got at one of the bull terriers and there was a litter of mongrels which they were going to have to have put down. We went to look at them and fell in love with one of them. 'No,' Dad said, 'no, no, no, no!' So we had her and called her Tally Taylforth, and she stayed with us for fourteen years. She looked like a Jack Russell, but she was the size of a bull terrier. She was like another baby for Mum.

Tally wouldn't eat dog food. She would eat chicken chow mein, beef curry and rice, anything but dog food. She would also do anything for a Polo. If you had one in your pocket or your bag she would root it out. In the end we gave up trying to give her tinned food and she would just eat whatever we had. On a Sunday she would gulp down a full roast – baked potato, Yorkshire pudding, carrots, gravy, the lot. She loved spaghetti, sucking up great strings of it, flicking the sauce over her face, just like that scene from *Lady and the Tramp*.

One day, when she was only a few months old, she contracted distemper, even though she had had all the injections, which meant that she was vomiting, had diarrhoea, weeping eyes and was frothing at the mouth. 'The best thing you can do,' the vet told me, 'is have her put down.'

'No.' I wouldn't hear of it. 'What else can I do for her?'

He gave me a list of instructions, which included feeding her boiled fish and chicken every few hours and getting fluid into her through tubes. We did everything the vet said. I went back to him two or three weeks later and Tally was looking quite strong. The vet was amazed. 'She won't die,' he told me, 'because you won't let her.'

While we were in our teens Kimmie became a Mormon. She did it at first because she was in love with Donny Osmond and she thought if she converted she might meet him. She then became actively involved in the church and is now married to a Mormon and very serious about it, never smoking or drinking alcohol, tea or coffee.

We used to get a lot of Jehovah's Witnesses coming round the flats, knocking on the doors and asking to come in for a chat. Kimmie said to Mum that if she just told them she was a Mormon they would go away and not bother her. One day they knocked on the door and Mum opened it with a cup of tea in one hand and a cigarette in the other. 'Oh, sorry, love, I'm Mormon!' she said and shut the door on their bemused expressions.

One year, I ordered a cake from a lady in Poplar for Mum and Dad's wedding anniversary. Kim and I went to fetch it in an old Datsun Cherry I had at the time, although neither of us knew the area. I have always been famous for getting lost the moment I turn out of the end of my road and this journey was no exception. It was getting late and becoming obvious that we were seriously lost as usual. We were both beginning to be flustered.

'We've got to retrace our steps,' Kimmie said. 'Take the next right and then we can turn round.'

I did as she said and we pulled into a cul-de-sac with a high brick wall across the end. On either side there were dark factory walls looming up above us, one with a metal fire escape zigzagging down the side. It was very gloomy and threatening and then the car stalled and refused to restart. The more I turned the key the more silent the engine remained.

'We mustn't panic,' Kim said, trying to calm both of us. 'Let's have a prayer.'

So we both closed our eyes and prayed. A second after we had said our 'amen's a man appeared on the fire escape, as if from nowhere, and came down to us. We didn't dare to wind down the window, but he signalled to me to open the bonnet from the inside. I did as he said and he lifted the hood. He fiddled about and the engine just started. He put the hood down again and as I went to wind the window down far enough to thank him he disappeared. Kim was absolutely certain it was an angel answering our prayers and she tells the story in church to this day.

After Allied Breweries I moved to a solicitor's office called Routh Stacey in Northampton Square, off Goswell Road, where I was to stay for about nine years. The company was in a very old building, with offices like rabbit hutches. It was a big firm with a lot of partners, all hidden away up little staircases with sloping floors and uneven windows. It was a lovely place to work. The people were friendly and I enjoyed the job. I loved typing. There's nothing better than getting a really good speed up when you are doing audio, and then at the end of the day looking at all the work you have done, seeing it all neatly laid out. I was doing conveyancing and we used to have to sew the documents up and wax them – this was in the days before word processors – and I have to admit that that did get a bit boring.

When it got close to my twenty-first birthday I decided I wanted a party, which meant I needed to earn an extra bit of money. So, after work at Routh Stacey's, I would do other jobs in the evenings. I used to work in the pub behind the bar, and I also did a stint in McDonald's. Although McDonald's seemed a little bit like slave labour I still quite enjoyed it. When you start you have to clean out the toilets and everything, which isn't much fun. One thing I will say for them is that they are a very clean business. When I had been there a little while the manager said he was going to try me 'on the window', which meant serving customers. This was what I wanted. We were all supposed to say 'Enjoy your meal' and 'Have a nice day', like Americans, but not many of the people working in this branch would do this. I loved it, the hammier the better. I must have sounded like a refugee from Disney World with my 'Have a nice day now' to every customer. I was really just having a laugh, but management thought it was great, upped my money and told me I could stay on the window.

And so life went on for a few years. When I was twenty I always imagined that by the time I was thirty or so I would be married with three children. It never occurred to me that I might have children without being married. I just took it for granted that it would happen that way. I was really looking forward to it, but I was also enjoying my life while I waited for 'Mr Right' to come along.

* * *

When Janice told Kim, Debbie, Ronnie and me that she was pregnant at nineteen by a chap she had been going out with for four years, we couldn't imagine how we would ever be able to break the news to Dad. We waited till we knew he would be down the bottom of the road at a darts match in the King's Head, where he was captain of the team, and we all went to see Mum. We just stood there, not knowing what to say. Eventually we blurted out the news, which she took quite well – I think she had already guessed – and then we left her to think how to break it to Dad. She decided that it would be a good idea to approach him while he was having a good time at the pub. She never normally went to the pub, but she pulled on her coat and strolled down the road. She went in, trying to look as if she had just dropped in for a shandy. Dad was surprised to see her, but bought her a drink and sat down beside her.

'I've got something to tell you, Ron,' she confessed.

'I thought there was something up. What is it?'

Eventually she found the words to tell him. He sat there in stunned silence for a while. Then he was all for throwing Janice out until Mum calmed him down. By the next day he was saying things like 'Well, I suppose it's time we became grandparents.' And when Jamie, their first grandchild, was born, they took him everywhere with them. On the day he was born we were all in the hospital room with bottles of champagne and they went on celebrating for days. The family had a new little star.

3

The Acting Bug

I had become interested in drama at school. I loved writing and English and I was always the first one wanting to get involved if there were any plays going on, really keen to be part of the excitement. I enjoyed going out on stage and being someone else, doing something different to normal, and I adored all the dressing up. Debbie became involved in classic acting, but I wasn't interested in that, with all those 'hath's, 'wilt's and 'thou's. (Debs also wrote a brilliant whodunnit with herself being murdered at the beginning, and she used to write episodes of *Batman* with herself as Catwoman, long before the famous Catwoman was even mentioned.)

I certainly never thought that I would end up making acting my career. At one stage I thought I would like to be a journalist because of all the contact that would give me with other people, chatting to them and getting involved in their lives. I told the careers teacher at school that was what I wanted to do.

'To be a journalist,' she warned me, 'you need to be prepared to be disliked. You'll have to go knocking on doors when someone has died and force your way in . . .'

I knew immediately that would not do for me. I am the sort of person who gets very distraught if I find out someone doesn't like me. It wouldn't matter if a million people said they did like me, I would do anything to win over the one who didn't. I may be an extrovert, but I have no confidence in myself. And now that I know more about what journalists have to do in order to get stories their editors will be happy with, I'm glad I didn't pursue that line of job hunting.

Kimmie was also into the theatre and it was her who first joined the Anna Scher Group in Islington. When I left school I found I was really missing the drama and Kim suggested that I come with her for some lessons in the evenings. The school was funded by the council, so it was very cheap, and the classes were held in a function room in a block of flats called Canonbury. This wasn't the sort of drama school where they would try to iron out your natural accent and make Shakespeare a compulsory part of the curriculum – it was the perfect place for the sort of work I wanted to do.

Having started as a drama teacher, Anna developed her business over the years into a big management company as well, handling the careers of many of the young people who came through her classes. At that time her star pupils were Pauline Quirke and Linda Robson, who had been going to Anna's since they were kids and were already starting to work professionally. They, of course, went on to be really successful in *Birds of a Feather*. Phil Daniels, who made his name in *Quadrophenia*, was in the same year, as was Ray Burdis, who later produced the film *The Kray Twins*. There were also a host of people like me and Sue Tully who went on to work in such programmes as *EastEnders*, *Casualty* and *The Bill*.

I went to Anna's two evenings a week for a while and then, when she felt I had reached a certain standard, it dropped to once a week, every Friday after work. By that time she had her own school in Barnsbury Road. I learned a lot there, doing improvisation, making a story up around three objects we were given, using masks, mirror images, dancing to music, having discussions. There would be twenty or so of us in a class and Anna would divide us into pairs, just giving us the first line of a scene – like asking the girl to say, 'I have to tell you, I'm pregnant', or a man saying to a woman, 'I'm leaving you' – and then we took it from there. Sometimes a group of us would be asked to do a play, and again we would be given only the first line. Anna would then talk about what we had done, criticising, making suggestions, helping us to think about our work and see ways in which we could have given it more depth.

We would talk about topical books and occasionally Anna would ask us to prepare a song or poem to recite the following week. I always went for the poem since I knew that singing was not my strongest subject. One week, however, she brought in a pianist and told us we all had to sing. When it came to my turn the others were all laughing because my knees were actually knocking together. Apart from that, acting was like a hobby for me and I loved it.

When I was about twenty-five Anna told me that I was now trained and didn't have to come every Friday any more. She said she would like to be my agent and see if she could get some professional bookings for me.

I had had a few tasters of professional acting along the way. After about six months of training I had been given a part in a 'Play for Today' called *Eleanor*. Pauline Quirke played Eleanor, an autistic child. Kimmie was hired to be one of her schoolfriends and volunteered my services as another, so I didn't even have to audition. I was given two lines: ''Ere, Miss' and 'I like that Rochester, Miss' (I was supposed to be reading *Jane Eyre* at the time). I really enjoyed myself, but it still didn't occur to me that I would ever be able to earn a full-time living from acting.

The next thing I was in was a play about a boxer, called *Fast Hands*. I played his fiancée and I had to break off the engagement and give his ring back when he was brain-damaged in a fight because I couldn't cope. Mum got so upset for the man when we were all sitting watching the play on television that she broke a stick of rock over my head, accusing me of being 'a horrible cow' and wanting to know 'how could you do that to him?'

I was in several other productions for children's television, and Kimmie got a part in a big production called *The Know- ledge*, which was about London taxi drivers and starred Nigel Hawthorne. I was happy to think that I would get the odd job like this and be able to go back to my proper work afterwards. It was like being paid to enjoy my hobby. My boss at the solicitors', Robert Neville, was really good about it all. When I was given a part in the remake of *The Rag Trade* he allowed me to have several months off work for the recording. I had two really good friends at the office called Philly and Mon (short for Monica) who used to cover for me and who have remained great friends to this day.

It's amazing that I have somehow developed a reputation in the media for being some sort of scarlet woman, because I've always been terrible at seduction scenes. I remember that in *The Rag Trade* I had to persuade Christopher Beeny's character to do something for me by using my 'feminine charms'. Every time I said the lines I went blood red and fluffed them, until the director was beginning to get quite angry. Christopher suggested that if I was embarrassed to look him in the eyes while I was whispering sweet nothings, I should concentrate my attention on the bridge of his nose. It was brilliant advice and I did the whole scene staring fixedly between his eyebrows.

My embarrassment at doing love scenes has not got any less, even after all these years. When Kathy first had to slip between the sheets with Phil in *EastEnders* I was wearing a body stocking with the straps pulled down, and leggings as well – I would have worn a balaclava if they'd let me. Then I turned over in the bed and saw that the props people had mounted a condom machine on the wall of Kathy's bedroom, with a specimen laid out on the bedside table. It was meant as a joke, but it didn't help my confidence! I don't know how other actors manage to do full love scenes; at least in *EastEnders* it doesn't get much further than a kiss and cuddle and then pulling the sheets up over our heads. It is a lot easier if you get on well with the other person and can have a laugh. I do get on particularly well with Steve McFadden, who plays Phil, even though he has a habit of doing things like lying on his back in the bed with a can of hairspray propping the sheet up between his legs to impress me! But I think that I will always feel funny about getting into bed with someone I'm not having a relationship with, even when there's a studio full of crew watching.

I was then cast in an episode of *Hi-de-Hi!* as a young girl camper who tries to seduce Mr Fairbrother in the bushes – even more embarrassing. The team on *Hi-de-Hi!* were so good to work with and so welcoming to us outsiders who just came for one episode. The filming was very nostalgic for me because it was all done at a holiday camp in Harwich that we used to go to as a family when I was little. Later on I was in panto with Jeffrey Holland, who played Spike in the programme. I did an episode of *Sink or Swim* with Peter Davison and a couple of *Shelleys*, one as a waitress and one as a nurse. In *Big Jim and the Figaro Club* I played 'The Tango Queen of Boghampton' and had to seduce Roland Curram in a court room.

Kimmie and I used to go to a lot of the same auditions, often with a group of other Anna Scher actresses like Pauline Quirke and Linda Robson, but there was never any back-biting or jealousy. Kim got a cameo part which we both went for, in *The Long Good Friday* with Bob Hoskins. Just before filming was due to start she went over to America for a holiday and there was an air strike on the day she was due to come home, which made her a week late. She rang the producers to tell them she wasn't going to be able to make it and reminded them that I had been at the audition as well. They rang me and I got the part. The character was called Sherry, which Dad thought was very funny: 'You can't even get away from drink when you're filming!' he teased.

Whenever I had auditions Robert Neville would let me go without making any fuss, provided I made up the time. Anna would always try to make the appointments for the evenings or lunchtimes so that I didn't have to ask too often. Kim did not have as much luck as me with bosses and each time she won an acting job she had to find a new job again after it finished. She reached the point of having to make a choice and decided to give up acting and join the police force. The funny thing was that she had been up for a part in *The Bill* and they had turned her down because she was 'too pretty' and they 'wanted to make the series seem realistic'. Although she was grateful for the security the force offered her, I think she did regret her decision. She was offered the main part in *London's Burning* when it was just a one-off play and turned it down. If she had known what a hit series it would turn into she might have decided differently. People think that successful actors and actresses have planned their careers from start to finish, but nearly everything happens by pure chance and one lucky break can change the rest of your life for you.

The first night Kim had to go out on patrol on her own, Ronnie wanted to follow her around to protect her. He soon realised, as we all did, that Kim was probably the best prepared of all of us to look after herself. She really does know how to stand up for herself: if anyone ever insults her or is rude, she won't just take it on the chin, she'll give as good as she gets – unlike me and Debbie, who both have more of an anything-for-a-quite-life kind of attitude.

To satisfy Kim's urge to perform she and Debbie – who was now working as a nursery nurse – used to tour around putting on cabaret performances for police charities. I used to join them sometimes, with all three of us singing 'Sisters, never were there such devoted sisters'. I loved doing that because they both had such good voices they could carry me along with them. Years later, when I was in *EastEnders*, there was a charity event called 'Trading Places Day', when well-known faces from television swapped jobs with other people. Kim challenged me and my friend Nula Conwell, who was playing WPC Martella in *The Bill*, to be policewomen for the day to raise money for a breast cancer research unit. We accepted the challenge and turned up at Holloway Police Station to be shown how to breathalyse drivers and dish out parking tickets.

Eventually my boss said that he really needed a full-time secretary, not someone who kept disappearing off for weeks on end, but they wanted to keep me in the company and he asked if I would mind working for other people in the same firm. So I moved on to the probate department for a couple of years. Then Robert Neville asked if I would go back to him because he hadn't been able to find anyone to replace me, which was a great compliment. After that I moved on to litigation for a while, so I gained a lot of experience of different aspects of legal work.

After nine years of working for Routh Stacey, another of the firm's partners called me in and sat me down. 'Listen,

Gillian,' he said, 'you have worked here for nine years now and been in almost every department. You are a top legal secretary and we really value you, but you are going to have to choose between your two careers. Do you want to be an actress or a secretary? You have to decide.'

I really didn't want to choose – I was afraid of giving up a good steady job for something which might never even happen. By now I was about twenty-seven and felt I was getting a bit old for Anna Scher's agency: in those days the industry tended to think of her as an agent for kids and teenagers, and the job offers for me had begun to slacken off. But when it came down to it, I enjoyed acting too much to give it up altogether. So the solicitors kept me on for as long as they could before I made up my mind to take the plunge and started temping for a while.

4

Leaving Home

Even now that we were mostly grown-up we still did an awful
lot of things together as a family. When we were little, Mum
had always told us about her childhood adventures with her
mother down in Kent when she used to go 'hopping' at a
place called Paddock Wood. Whole gangs of them used to
go off for a few weeks at a time, living in wooden sheds
and picking the hops during the days, while the kids ran
wild in the fields. 'Let's go and find this Paddock Wood,
then,' we said one day, 'and see where you used to work.'
Debbie's husband had a Bedford van which we all piled into
and headed down into Kent. I don't think we ever found the
place, but when we thought we were close we got out for a
walk in the countryside. We found a bunch of trees around
a deep dip, one of which had a rope tied to it, obviously so
that kids could swing across. We couldn't resist this. All the
others made spectacular Tarzan jumps across the dip, landing
neatly on the other side, then it came to my turn.

'Geronimo!' I shouted, lifting off and heading out into
mid-air. Like a character from _Tom and Jerry_ I went flat
into the mud on the other side, leaving a perfect imprint
of my face and my outstretched arms and legs. Mum was
frightened that I had hurt myself, but the rest of them were
beside themselves with hysterics.

When the landlord at the local pub, John, said he wanted

to raise some money for charity, we all volunteered to dress up as characters from *St Trinian's* for the evening. Dad went as George Cole's spiv character, Kim and a couple of her friends went as big girls in suspenders and torn tights, while Debbie and I were young girls with our hair in bunches, freckles painted on our noses and skirts down to our ankles. People could have their pictures taken with us for donations. Dad was running a tote, taking bets on 'Deb's Delight' and 'Gill's Folly', and we kidnapped John and held him to ransom – but no one would pay any money for him, so we had to let him go.

I finally left home when I was twenty-seven, moving to a flat in Highbury. I knew it was time to do something when I found myself telling Janice off for staying out late, sounding just like Mum and Dad. Mum came with me to buy some furniture for my first home. Once we were in the shop I started talking to the salesman about a double bed.

'What do you want a double bed for?' Mum hissed while the man was looking the other way.

'Mum, I'm twenty-seven, it just might be nice if I had a boyfriend or something . . .'

'Just don't let your father know you've got a double bed. There's no reason for it.'

I suppose I was pretty unusual in my lack of worldly experience. Most of my generation left home as soon as they could, either living with someone, marrying someone or having a string of partners. My first boyfriends had mostly been nice boys who were still living at home with their mums and dads, just like me. When I was about twenty-five I met Tele, who had a place of his own. After we had been going out for a while he asked if I would stay over. When I suggested it at home they said definitely not. It was simply out of the question. I don't think any of the others would have asked for permission in the first place and they certainly wouldn't have taken any notice of the answer. I don't know why, but I had always been the one who did as I was told. I always respected Mum and Dad and so when they said something was a fact I believed them. If they said it wasn't right, then it wasn't right. I was very worried about what they thought of me, desperate not to hurt or anger anyone. After a while I began to think that perhaps the situation was becoming a bit ridiculous. There I was, twenty-six by then, and not able to stay out overnight if I wanted to. Plucking up my courage I took the giant step of disobeying them and I stayed the night with Tele. It resulted in me being sent to Coventry for a week. When I got in on the Sunday after my daring act of defiance I made myself a cup of tea and put it down on the side in the kitchen. My brother Ronnie came in and went to pick up the cup.

'Don't touch that,' Dad warned him. 'Gillian's just drunk out of it.' I went to my bedroom and cried my eyes out. I couldn't bear it that he actually thought of me like that, that I was no longer his little girl.

The others were always teasing me about how prudish I was. I used to think that ideally you shouldn't have sex until you were married and then you should have children and do everything properly. I couldn't even swear like the others, preferring to spell the words out rather than say them. Whenever I went on holiday with my sisters or girlfriends they would happily go topless on the beach, but I could never bring myself to do it. I have always been particularly self-conscious about my bust, thinking that I looked too much like a bloke and people would laugh at me if I went topless. Apart from that I could never see the point in tanning parts of the body which were always covered up anyway.

It wasn't that I hadn't had sex before Tele. My first time had been when I was about twenty. My boyfriend at the time, Peter, had come over to stay with me while my parents were away on holiday because there had been a prowler in the area. We made love and I felt so guilty afterwards that I wept. It didn't help that he called me 'Brenda' at the critical moment, either. I was very naive about sex because it had been such a taboo subject with Mum. She used to tell us that if we wanted to know anything we just had to ask her, but whenever we did ask she'd say, 'What do you want to know that for?' So I learned, rather inaccurately, from other girls at school. It wasn't something that really interested me, I just assumed I would do it when the time came. I really didn't want to think about it until later on. I used to kiss and cuddle with boys on the doorstep, saying goodnight after a date, just because I thought that was what you were supposed to do, but it never occurred to me to go any further. Sex was something to giggle about, not something to *do*.

I did, however, enjoy having boyfriends because it meant we could go down to the pub with other couples and all the boys could sit at one table, talking about football, and the girls could sit together at another and have a laugh. When I did finally get round to having sex I couldn't really see what all the fuss was about; I would have been quite happy to live without it. It never has been the most important aspect of any of my relationships with men. If it's been good that has been a bonus. The most important thing to me is to have a friend to come home to, someone I can have a laugh and a joke with, and I'm often happier at the end of the day just having a kiss and a cuddle, feeling that warmth and security. I always imagined that I would meet the right person and remain happily married all my life, like Mum and Dad, who had been together since they were fifteen, and like my aunt and uncle and my grandparents, too. I wanted it to be just like it was in all the old movies.

I read a letter in a magazine recently from a girl saying she was twenty-three and still a virgin and she was 'so depressed'. I can't understand that. I think it's something she should be really proud of, and pleased that she is saving all that for the right man.

Peter, my first real boyfriend, worked as a postman and we went out for a couple of years. When I passed my driving test he bought me an old Anglia Estate for £90 so that I could get about. I was so proud of my first car. Peter was very sweet and I was fond of him, but our life seemed to fall into a routine of just going down to the pub every evening and I got a bit fed up with it. I decided – foolishly – that I needed a bit more excitement, and that's when things started to go wrong. In my experience, men who offer a bit of excitement also offer a lot of heartache to go with it.

I met Dave in a pub called the Dun Cow in the Old Kent Road. I was there with Nula Conwell, whom I had met at Anna Scher's. She was a few years younger than me and an amazing character. She came on holiday with me when we had just met and when she was still only fifteen – I couldn't believe that anyone had parents who would allow such a thing – and we've stayed firm friends ever since.

One evening on the holiday some boys invited us to go skinny dipping. In our innocence we went back to the hotel and put our costumes on under our clothes. When we met the boys on the beach later and they stripped off their underwear we nearly died of shock. They explained to us what skinny dipping meant and we explained that unless they kept their bottoms on we were going straight back to the hotel. We all ended up having a very nice – and modest – swim together.

When we got to the Dun Cow, Dave was working on the door. During the evening we got chatting and he noticed that we came from the other side of the river and guessed we didn't know the area, so he suggested a club we should go on to. He made it sound good, so we went along. We had only been there a short time when he turned up again. We talked some more and he suggested that he and I should go out together. We used to go to a lot of good pubs and clubs, often staying out till late, which caused a bit of friction at home, but life with Dave was all very new and exciting and I was having a good time.

We went out for several months. He used to get me to pick him up in my car at the end of his road and drop him off there afterwards. I didn't think anything of it until one night he told me he was going to a pub but I couldn't come.

'But I've been there before,' I protested.

'Well, there's a special night on tonight, so you can't.'

I thought, why not? But then I put it out of my mind. After a while he suggested that I stay out all night with him at a party and, taking my courage in both hands, I agreed. I didn't tell Mum and Dad about the plan, knowing what their reaction would be. We went to a good party and stayed there until early in the morning. When I got home mid-morning there was only Janice in the flat.

'What are you doing out of school?' I asked.

'Mum's looking for you,' she warned me. 'She's gone up to the police station.'

'Oh my God!' I phoned the police station and told the sergeant who I was. 'Is my mother there?'

'She's on her way back now,' he said, 'and if I was you I'd get out now.'

'What's happened?'

'She came in and told us her daughter was missing, so we started taking down all the details. When we asked her how old you were, and she said twenty-four, I'm afraid we started laughing. We suggested that she went back home and if you still didn't turn up to let us know later on. She wasn't too happy about it.'

As I put the phone down I saw Mum's silhouette in the glass of the front door and I felt myself breaking out in a cold sweat. I opened the door for her and her first words were 'Pack your bags, you're out!'

'I don't want to go,' I was pleading. 'Please let me stay.'

'Well, you'd better phone your dad up at work and ask him if you can stay.'

I got on the phone to Dad and he told me we'd 'talk about it when he got home'. By that time everyone had calmed down and I was beginning to see the funny side. I guess by staying at home for so much longer than everyone else I prolonged the agony for my parents of watching me grow away from them and start to make my own mistakes. Usually all that sort of thing takes place after the children have left home and the parents don't find out until it's too late to do anything about it. I behaved myself impeccably for a few weeks to let the dust settle.

The phone went one evening at home. 'Is there someone there who knows a bloke called Dave Hammond?' a woman's voice asked.

'Yeah, I know him,' I said.

'Well, who are you?' the voice asked.

'Who are you?' I wanted to know. I didn't like the tone of her voice.

'Look, love, I've been living with Dave for years and I'm about to have his child.'

'Sorry?' I couldn't take it in. As I struggled to listen to what she was saying it all started to fit together, why I had never been to his house, why he sometimes couldn't be seen with me. How could I have been so stupid? It was all so obvious.

When I next spoke to Dave he convinced me that this woman was deluded and their relationship was all over, and I believed him. I had led such a sheltered life I always took people at face value. When he gave me an explanation for everything the woman had said I thought, 'Fair enough, that sounds likely,' and put the whole thing out of my mind. I think I might even have felt sorry for him for having this woman messing about with his life. But when I told my parents what Dave had said they were less impressed.

'Leave it out, girl,' Dad said, 'chuck him in. Don't be so stupid, you're so naive.'

'No, honest, Dad, he's explained it all . . .'

Then Dave started to get a bit slap-happy when we were having a row. It was the first time I had ever come across a man who could be violent towards women and it came as a shock, but I thought it must be partly my fault for upsetting him. After the first argument I had a real shiner. I went into work and told everyone I had fallen and hit my eye on a window-sill. I phoned Mum and told her that she might notice something different about me when I got home.

'You've had your hair cut,' she guessed. Later she told me that Dad had guessed right the moment she told him about my call. It must all have seemed so predictable to them, but I was learning each lesson for the first time and it was a disillusioning experience.

When I got in I took off the sunglasses I was using to cover up the damage and Dad looked at me with no expression on his face. As he walked away I saw that his fists were bunched up. He kept hitting the armchair, hissing, 'Where is he? Where is he?'

When my brother Ronnie saw me he was all for going to get a hammer to deal with Dave. I told them not to worry, and that I had finally seen sense and wouldn't be seeing him any more, and eventually they calmed down. Dave rang and begged me to see him just once more because he had a present for me, to make up for what he had done. I met him at the end of the road and he gave me the present – a pair of sunglasses! This time I was definitely unimpressed.

He still managed to convince me that he was genuinely sorry for what he had done and begged me to go on seeing him. Like an idiot I did. I suppose it was because all my boyfriends before had been really nice boys – Dave was so different and that made it exciting; I wanted to believe him just so that things wouldn't go back to being boring again. The trouble was that all the boys I had met who would have made sweet husbands and who were keen on me always seemed to be the ones who let me make all the decisions, so I got bored very quickly. The ones who were more decisive and who wanted to lead their own lives first, with their women fitting in where possible, tended to be the ones who might give women a hard time. I used to think there was something very attractive about men like this, and even though I was beginning to realise that they were not the sort of people who settle down for the type of romantic marriage I was dreaming of, they always seemed to be the more interesting ones. I dare say this all explains why I'm still unmarried now.

Nula and I used to go out together a lot about the time I got my own place and when someone invited us to a fancy-dress party in a pub we jumped at the chance. I dressed up as a woman from a harem and Nula was a South American dancer, complete with all the headgear. We drove out to the pub, which we hadn't been to before, and waited to make sure a few other people had gone in before us. By about half past nine we still hadn't seen anyone go in wearing anything except ordinary clothes. 'We've got the wrong place,' I kept saying. 'We can't go in there dressed like this.'

A boy was walking past, so I called him over and asked him to go inside to the off-licence bit of the premises and get us a couple of lagers. Once we had downed them we had a bit more Dutch courage. It was past ten and we were getting our fair share of funny looks from passers-by anyway, so we decided to take the plunge and went in. Inside we found the place was packed with people in fancy dress – they had all brought their clothes with them and changed upstairs. We stayed until about four in the morning and then went to Guzelgun, a Turkish restaurant in the Essex Road that we all used to go to, and had a meal. By the time we came out it was about half past six and the birds were singing.

'Let's get a cab,' I suggested.

'No,' Nula said, 'it's not worth it. We'll take a bus.'

'Whichever comes along first.' I agreed on a compromise, just as a bus came round the corner, crammed with cleaners on their way to work. Having us come on board dressed like that must have made their day. I only had a couple of stops and then had to leave Carmen Miranda to fend for herself. It was great to have that freedom at last.

5

On Safari

When I got the job as a presenter for *On Safari* I truly thought it might lead to something. It was a slapstick children's show, which I really loved doing. The host was Chris Biggins, who had actually suggested me for the part when they asked him for a few names of people he might like to work with. I had worked with him before on a comedy show with Liza Goddard called *Watch This Space*, in which I played the secretary, Brenda – that name again!

That series had been such a happy experience for all of us. It was set in an advertising agency; Biggins, as he calls himself, was the boss and Liza and Peter Blake were a husband-and-wife team who worked for him. There was also a character played by Leo Dolan who ran the messages and did the odd jobs. We were a really close team and we had enormous fun making it – we used to laugh so much at rehearsals we could hardly get the lines out. They only ever made one series, so I guess the audiences didn't think it was as funny as we did. Leo came up to *EastEnders* to play the part of a man who wanted to provide a buffet service in the café a few years later, and the moment I saw him I burst out laughing, before he had even opened his mouth. We spent the whole time swapping stories about *Watch This Space*.

I love doing comedy. It was what I was always best at at Anna Scher's, but it is very hard work because you have to get the laughs or the whole thing dies. With straight drama there isn't that immediate test of success or failure. People may come up to you afterwards and say they liked or didn't like something you did, but by then it's all months in the past. With comedy you know immediately if the jokes are falling flat and there is nothing you can do about it. I was really itching to try my hand at something a bit more serious, but something which had humour in it as well as drama. Unfortunately you can't choose what you are asked to audition for, and if you are known for comedy roles, that is what you will be offered. I was so pleased to be working at all that I never complained.

Chris Biggins is a really fun bloke to work with, we just laughed and joked all the time. He kept saying, 'On Safari will be your big break, Gilly. If it didn't happen with The Rag Trade it must happen with this. It must lead to something. Your agent should be really pushing you now that you're on this.' But at the end of it nothing happened. The series went on for two years and when it finished I went back to work at my proper job. Every time I thought I had got my foot on the first rung of the ladder I would discover that I had climbed straight back down again. I often wondered if Kimmie had made the right decision by getting out of the business, but something kept me hoping and the encouragement of friends like Biggins played a big part in that.

I went down to see him in panto one Christmas. Jack Tinker, the theatre critic from the Daily Mail, came down with his friend and we went back to Biggins's home afterwards with a bunch of the dancers. We sat up nearly all night and they kept encouraging me to tell more jokes and stories. Years later Jack took me to lunch at the Ivy restaurant in London to interview me for the Mail and he remembered that evening. He wrote one of the nicest pieces anyone has ever written about me, saying I was one of the funniest women he knew. I was really touched.

Biggins and I often used to go to things together. He took me to a theatre preview one night and Cilla Black was there with her husband Bobby. Biggins knows them well and the four of us went on to dinner at a restaurant in Covent Garden called Orso. While we were there Shirley Bassey arrived and came over to talk to Cilla. I was very impressed by all this big-time stuff.

Back in the real world, however, I still had to earn a living in between acting jobs and so I was temping. I have always been obsessively conscientious about any work that I do, and in one job this obsession was my downfall. I was working for a big company in an office block in the City somewhere. I had just finished a day's word processing and I had a lot of printing to do. It was Friday evening and my last day there, so I was determined to finish the job and have it on the bosses' desks ready for the Monday morning. By half past six I had it all completed and I got ready to leave. As I came out of the room, however, I discovered that all the lights were switched off. Turning the odd one back on I made my way downstairs through the eerie, silent corridors, only to discover that all the doors were locked and, as far as I could tell, there was no one else in the building. With a rising feeling of panic I went back up to the office I had been working in and phoned Mum.

'I'm locked in!'

'Stay where you are, Gill,' she said. 'I'll call the police.'

'Hold on, Mum.' This brought me to my senses for a moment. 'Let me have one more try at finding a key, then I'll call you back.'

She agreed reluctantly and I ventured back downstairs, my heart pounding in my chest by now. I tried every door and looked everywhere I could think of for a key. Nothing. I felt very trapped. I made my way back upstairs and called Mum back.

'Well, that's long enough,' she said. 'I'll send the police to get you out. You go down to the front door and wait.'

I did as I was told and made my way back to reception. As I sat there, waiting very nervously, I looked up and saw a little box on the wall with a key in it and the message 'In emergency break glass.' I decided that I was going to have to do it – I couldn't bear the thought of being locked in a moment longer. I took one of my shoes off and raised it above my head to use the heel as a hammer. At that moment the handle on the front door turned – someone was coming in from the outside. 'My God,' I thought, 'burglars.' Still with my shoe poised to strike I moved behind the door, waiting to pounce on the intruder. A few moments later they were inside and I leapt out with a blood-curdling scream, coming face to face with a cleaner who was screaming even louder than me. When we had both calmed down enough to speak I had to race to find a phone to call Mum and get her to stop the police coming to my rescue.

Later on I joined a travel agency as PA to the boss, Terry Stallard. It was a brilliant job because he asked me to be his driver as well, so I got out and about with him. It meant I had a great social life, taking him to all the big travel agents' events. I liked working in the office as well. All the customers were always so nice and friendly because they were thinking about their holidays when they called.

I did still get some auditions. At one stage in the early 1980s I was up for a part in the first big Lynda La Plante series, *Widows*. I did a reading and they told me they were really happy and the job was virtually mine. I was very excited because it would have been a great part and the series was obviously going to be a big hit. In the end I didn't get it and when I watched the programme later I could see that the girl who won it was much better than I would have been. The character was supposed to be the daughter of a Cockney who was trying to better herself and be a model. I would have been all right as the daughter round the markets, but I didn't have the face or the figure for a girl who was making it in modelling.

Although I liked my secretarial work I was disappointed to think that my acting career just wasn't going to take off. I thought about all sorts of different things I could do, including the possibility of going into the police force with Kimmie. I particularly liked the idea of riding the horses. I applied and got a WPC to come out and talk to us, but she told me that if I joined the force I wouldn't be able to go on with my acting because I wouldn't be allowed to have any other source of income. I still didn't want to give up acting altogether, so that was the end of that idea.

When I first thought about joining the police I asked a couple of policemen how I should go about it, and confided that what I really wanted to be was 'a mounted policewoman'.

'I don't think,' one of them said with a grin, 'you'll have any trouble achieving that.'

I thought, what's he talking about? When I asked a friend later and told him the story he explained what I'd said.

Even though I had left home officially, I still spent most of my time off with the family. When Mum won £170 on the pools she announced that she was going to hire a caravan at Weymouth and anyone who wanted to come down would be welcome. Kimmie and her first husband Rod went, and me and Debbie and Mum and Dad. There was one double room for Mum and Dad and then a tiny second room with bunk beds. Debbie and I were going to sleep on a table which pulled out to become a spare double bed. Rod went to undress in the room with the bunks, but unfortunately as he took his trousers down he got his arms stuck between the bed and the wall and was wedged tight, unable to move in any direction. We all heard his cries for help because Debbie and I were setting our bed up in the other room and Kimmie was helping us. She went in to help him first and then called us in to see him, jammed in the room with his trousers at half mast. We all became too weak with laughter to help him. Eventually Kimmie crawled in between his legs to try to dislodge him while Debbie and I stumbled back to our bed and collapsed on to it in hysterics. We must have landed with too much force because our bed tried to turn itself back into a table, folding us in half with our knees round our ears. Now it was our turn to shout for help, when we could get our breath from laughing, but Kimmie couldn't get back out of their bedroom now and could only stick her head out through Rod's legs. Mum and Dad had to come back out of their room to sort us all out.

About this time my nan died and Mum and Dad were heart- broken. Mum even lost her voice for a while. We all felt the loss terribly, nothing was ever going to be the same again. She and Grandad had always been like another set of parents to us kids.

During this period I was going out with Tele, which was the most serious relationship of my life so far. We came very close to making a go of it, but we had too many different ideas and we eventually decided to end it. There were times when I was really keen on him and times when he was really keen on me, but sadly those times never seemed quite to overlap. I'm glad to say that we have managed to stay very good friends indeed.

I started to go out with a boy called Peter who was in the building trade. After we had been dating for about six weeks he invited me out for the evening of my birthday in August and said we would be going to a restaurant.

'What shall I wear?' I asked.

'Oh,' he sounded casual, 'just wear something smart. I'm going to wear a bow tie and a dinner jacket.'

So I got myself all dressed up, with my hair up and all the make-up. Peter came to collect me. 'Before we go to the restaurant,' he said, 'there's a block of flats at Kenwood I just want to look at, do you mind if we stop off?'

So we were in the middle of Hampstead Heath on this nice summer's evening and we came across a man dressed as a waiter, standing beside a great long table which had been laid out for an elegant open-air meal for two. A bottle of champagne was cooling in an ice bucket on a side table.

'Oh, look at that,' I said. 'What's going on there?'

He steered me over to the table and the waiter came forward and greeted me by name. Peter had set the whole thing up for my birthday surprise. I couldn't believe it – it was like having *This Is Your Life* sprung on you. I went bright red and protested as they sat me down. The waiter produced this wonderful meal from a catering van parked amongst the trees, including a complete lobster. People were wandering past, smiling, pointing, saying how romantic it looked and one woman asked if we were filming a commercial. A dog came over and just sat by the table, looking up at us with big mournful eyes, hoping for a few scraps. After a few glasses of champagne I started to get into the swing of it and at the end of the meal Peter said my present would be an engagement ring and asked me to marry him. It was so sweet of him and such a wonderful gesture, but I just wasn't ready at that time to think about anything permanent.

All the boyfriends my sisters and I had became friends of the family because Dad always insisted in the early days that if we had a date the boy had to come to the house to pick us up – none of that meeting under a clock somewhere. I went out with some really nice blokes in those days and nearly all of them have remained good friends with the family even now they are married with families of their own. They all came from the same community as us and, with one or two exceptions, had the same values as we did. None of them, however, quite managed to persuade me to take the plunge into marriage, even though it was something I really wanted to do. Perhaps my time was too occupied with my work, family and friends, or perhaps I had just set my romantic sights too high and no one quite managed to live up to my expectations.

Not every outing I had with my family went well. Quite soon after I started working on *EastEnders* Debbie and I were out at a pub in Dalston on Christmas Eve with a friend called Penny. We left the pub at about half past five, when it was already dark. Debbie has always been the nervous one of the family. When we were young I used to take great pleasure in winding her up when there were horror films on television. We were watching a Dracula film once where the Count kept appearing in a puff of smoke and Debbie went out to the bathroom. I ran to the kitchen, filled a hot-water bottle and hid behind the bathroom door. When she came out I let out a ghoulish shriek and a cloud of steam from the bottle. Poor Debbie nearly had a nervous breakdown. This particular evening I was walking ahead, towards the car, with Debbie and Penny walking behind me, when a boy came up and pulled me round, grabbing at a gold chain and cross which I was wearing. The chain broke and as I looked round to give him an earful I saw five other boys coming up behind him with menacing looks in their eyes. 'Oh, come on, lads,' I said, 'it's Christmas Eve,' but the next thing I knew the leader had punched me in the eye, thrown me back against the car and was trying to get my handbag. I held on to it, struggling to fight him off. Debbie came running up, shouting, and one of his mates head-butted her above the eye. She went down with blood everywhere. The boys panicked and ran off, grabbing Penny's handbag. I was so angry I chased after them, shouting abuse. A woman who was passing called me back to Debbie, who was lying on the pavement crying out for me, and I came to my senses. The police turned up and we sorted Debbie out. Penny went with her to the hospital and I set off home to let them know what had happened. When Dad saw the state of my eye and heard that Debs was in hospital he went mad – someone had dared to touch two of his little girls!

'Take me there,' he said. 'Show me where you went.'

He rounded up Ronnie and a couple of other friends, one of whom was a karate instructor, and we set off like characters from a Michael Winner film. Dad was stopping every black man he came across, asking me if he was one of the gang. I was completely dazed and couldn't have recognised anyone anyway. We came to a club called the Four Aces which looked a bit rough. Dad went up to a man playing snooker. 'You,' he said.

The man turned slowly and looked up. 'Yeah?'

'You seen any blokes in here with a handbag?'

The man straightened himself up and Dad hardly came to his shoulder. 'No, man,' he shook his head, 'I ain't seen no one.'

By this time Ronnie and the others had caught us up and seen who Dad was talking to. They tried to get him out, but he was reluctant to go, feeling sure that he was on to something. 'See my girl.' He dragged me forward, pointing to my eye, which had virtually closed up by then. 'See what they've done to her?' When Ronnie and his mate eventually got Dad outside they told him that he had just been facing up to one of the country's top boxers on his night off. Not that Dad cared, he would have faced up to anyone that night.

Debbie came out of hospital the next day with a bandage round her head and we all sat round the Christmas lunch table looking like extras from *Casualty*. I had some filming to do a few days later, by which time my eye had turned a horrible mauve colour, so the make-up girls just used mauve eye shadow on the other eye to match them up.

6

The Big Break

'Those of you who get parts in this series,' the producer warned us, 'will become household names.'

The warning went in one ear and out the other as far as I was concerned. I didn't think I would get the part and I certainly couldn't imagine what it would mean to be a household name. People promise you all sorts of things when they are planning new projects. Everyone has the highest hopes and they always think that whatever they are doing will make you a star. By this time I had been around long enough to take all their promises with a pinch of salt. The auditions were for a new soap opera the BBC was planning to launch to rival ITV's *Coronation Street*, which was the most popular programme in the country. I really liked the idea of getting into a long-running soap opera and this one seemed like the perfect opportunity, being set amongst working-class London families – something I knew a thing or two about. I deliberately didn't let my hopes get too high, but I couldn't help being excited.

When I went home and tried to impress Mum and Dad with the prediction that I might soon be a 'household name', Dad was as matter-of-fact as usual. 'Household name?' he muttered. 'Like Domestos, you mean?'

'Yeah, Dad, something like that.'

The producers, Julia Smith and Tony Holland, whose idea

the series was, had been down to Anna Scher's to watch a workshop one evening, knowing that they would find plenty of authentic young Londoners there, and had asked some of us to go for auditions. Initially they were thinking of me for the part of Sue in the café.

'We aren't thinking of Sue for you any more,' Julia told me when I went up to the BBC for the second audition, 'we're thinking of Kathy Beale. The only trouble is we don't think you're old enough because you need to have an eighteen-year-old son.'

'I'm nearly twenty-nine,' I said. 'I'll have a couple of rough nights.'

We tried a few things like putting my hair up, while Tony Holland sat there with a calculator trying to work out when I might have had this baby. The next time I was called up Wendy Richard was there with Bill Treacher, who was going to play her husband, Leslie Grantham and another actress who was originally going to play Angie, and Peter Dean, who was going to play Kathy's husband, Pete Beale. Letitia Dean, who was to play Sharon, was also there from the beginning, as were Anna Wing (Lou Beale) and Adam Woodyatt (Pete and Kathy's son Ian). Other major characters at the beginning were Ethel, Dr Legg, and Sue and Ali in the café. We did lots of readings and when it came to about four o'clock Julia Smith said that I could go. But the others were still there. I thought that was it and I left feeling very depressed. I was upset because they seemed such a nice team and I thought I had got on really well with everyone. It felt a bit like a repeat of losing *Widows*. I phoned Mum.

'How did you get on?' she asked.

'Well, the others are still there,' I told her.

'Oh, never mind, darling, something better will come along.'

I went back to the travel agents' the next day and got on with my job. Two weeks later, having forgotten all about it, I received a phone call and I heard Anna Scher's voice singing 'Congratulations' down the line.

'What?'

'You got the part as Kathy!'

I couldn't believe it. I was just twenty-nine and Kathy was supposed to be thirty-six, but I'd been given the part. I felt so lucky because I knew that I had got in by the skin of my teeth. Julia Smith later wrote in her book on the making of *EastEnders* that they saw more people for the part of Kathy Beale than for any other character.

That evening I phoned Mum and Dad. 'I've got some really good news, I'm coming round this evening to celebrate.'

I went there straight from work with two bottles of champagne. I cracked one open and handed the glasses round.

'So what's the good news?' Mum asked, taking a glass even though she never drinks.

'I got the part of Kathy Beale.'

'Oh.' She looked crestfallen for a moment. 'I thought you were going to tell us you'd got engaged.'

I knew how pleased they all were for me really, even though Grandad said he couldn't always watch the programme because it clashed with *Emmerdale Farm*. 'That's marvellous, isn't it,' I teased him back, 'your granddaughter losing out to a load of bleeding sheep.'

A week before we were due to start recording, after we had been rehearsing and getting to know our characters for several months, we were told that Anita Dobson was taking over the part of Angie. She would have about six episodes to learn in a couple of days. Apparently the producers didn't think the chemistry was working between the first actress and Leslie. They were anxious to make a big impact right from the start. They didn't want to start off low-key, as often happened with soaps, and let the characters grow on the audience – they wanted to grab people's attention from the first episode. Angie and Den had major scenes in those early episodes and we all wondered how anyone could manage, being thrown in at the deep end like this.

Within two days Anita knew every line and when she was filming a scene in which she was drunk and Den had to carry her upstairs, she started making up her own bits. We all burst into spontaneous applause at the end of the scene, she was so good and the chemistry was perfect – there was real electricity between them. Now we could see why the producers had taken such a big risk. From then on Den and Angie became the stars of the show, so much so that now, ten years on, they are packaging videos of early episodes and calling them 'The Den and Angie Years'.

When they both left we all wondered who could ever take their place, and then along came Pat (Pam St Clement) and Frank (Mike Reid). Pam had been in the show almost from the start; on screen she played my husband Pete's ex-wife, but off screen we were the best of mates! Mike was already well known for his stand-up comedy and he took to working behind the bar as if he had been doing it all his life. It is sometimes difficult for actors who do a lot of stage work to tone their performances down for the small screen. On stage you need to be larger than life with big expressions and gestures. Both Anita and Mike had to relearn their craft a bit when they started in *EastEnders* so that they didn't look over the top, but their experience of stage work gave them such confidence and charisma that they always held the attention of the audience when they were on.

Anita became a good friend and I always enjoyed being with her. I used to go out sometimes in a group with Anita,

Letitia Dean, Sue Tully (who played Michelle) and Sandy
Ratcliffe (who got the part of Sue in the café and who I
got on very well with). On one of these outings we went to
Joe Allen's, a hamburger restaurant in Covent Garden where
a lot of show-business people go in the evenings. It's a very
noisy, lively place. There was a table full of men next to us
and we got talking. We were all pretty merry by this time and
I started hamming it up as if I was a Madame Fifi out with her
call girls, telling the men that if they 'wanted to speak to any
of my girls they had to go through me'. We were all larking
about and in such high spirits we didn't want the evening
to end; Sandy went home, but the rest of us went back to
Anita's place in the East End. (This was in the days before
Anita met Brian May from Queen.) There was only one bed
in the flat, so Anita, Letitia and I got in together and Sue
was on the floor. Anita had the room lit with a candle, but
when she blew it out so we could get some sleep none of us
could stop giggling. We were like a bunch of schoolgirls in a
dormitory after lights out. We were just settling down when
the phone rang, but we couldn't find it in the dark. Anita
had to grope around for some matches to light the candle
and we were sure that it would stop ringing by the time we
got organised. Eventually we answered it and it was Sandy,
ringing to tell us she had got home safely, which set us all
off into hysterics again. God knows what stories the media
could have dreamed up the next day if they had known we
were three in a bed with a candle!

Another group of us used to include Linda Davidson, who
played the punk Mary in the series, and Hilary Nash, who was
a dresser for Anita and me and has now come back to do props.
We used to call ourselves the 'Dolly Dewdrop Club' and had
some great times.

As well as the official BBC parties, the cast often organise their own get-togethers. One Christmas Haluk, who played Ali's brother Mehmet in the show, arranged for us all to go to a Turkish restaurant. There was a belly dancer who gyrated around having money pushed into her clothes by the audience. When she had finished she gave me her bells to have a go and, ably encouraged by the rest of the party, I ended up on the table having everything from beer mats to empty fag packets shoved into my pockets and what there is of my 'cleavage'.

When I'd finished I went to the toilets to tidy myself up and found June Brown (Dot Cotton) in the middle of undressing herself.

'What are you doing, June?' I asked in surprise.

'I had to get these thermals off, dear,' she said waving her underwear at me, 'I had no idea it would be so hot here. Look, I'm pouring with sweat!' Once she got back outside she was down on the dance floor with the rest of us. She was always good fun to have around.

Working in a soap opera is very largely a matter of routine and being part of a team. We think of ourselves as a firm, with new people joining the regulars all the time just like in any other business. When you have been in a series for some time the writers get to know your personality and begin to write for you a bit more, so the characters sometimes begin to grow more like the actors playing them. But at the beginning we were all unknown quantities and we had to let the writers and directors tell us what we were going to be doing and how our characters would be developed.

The first thing that happens is a script of three new episodes at a time is posted into your dressing room. These episodes will be going out on the air in five or six weeks' time. The front of the script lists all the technical and production staff who are going to be involved. It also has the sunset times for outside filming. The filming is divided up between what is going to happen outside on the lot and what will be shot inside in the studio. Each episode has eighty or ninety pages of script in it. I usually read the new script through quickly in order to find out what is going on with all the other characters before marking up my bits. Some of the others can remember the directions which the directors give them, but I always write them on the scripts just in case. I also cover them in doodles during the endless hours of waiting around.

In any one week we might be working on as many as nine different episodes, especially now that the programme is going out three times a week; rehearsing some, doing studio shots on others and location shooting on others. More normally we have six episodes at a time in our heads, which is an awful lot to stay on top of. I learn my lines the night before filming. Because things are shot out of sequence it is sometimes difficult to remember what is supposed to have happened in the plot so far. Are you, for instance, supposed to know that the man you are talking to is having an affair with someone else, or are you supposed to find that out in a couple of days' time?

Anyone who has ever appeared in a soap for a long period will tell you just how hard you have to work. An actor who appears on stage in the West End every night has the physical strain of giving a performance but, with perhaps a few minor changes, the show will remain the same and so he can use his technique to produce good performances without having to think about a whole lot of new material he has only just found out about. Actors making films have the same problem as we do of shooting scenes out of order, but a film project seldom lasts for more than a few months, with a lot of time for preparation before shooting starts, whereas a soap opera goes on for years with virtually no time for preparation. Some actors avoid soaps because they feel it is too much like having a normal job, but with a lot of extra pressures.

Sometimes I think that working under this sort of pressure can actually help the spontaneity of the show. I have been in programmes where we might have a week or ten days of rehearsal before filming, which can lead to us looking a bit over-rehearsed when it comes to the final shooting. On *EastEnders*, unless it is a really difficult scene, we probably only go through it once or twice before filming, which makes it very fresh.

There are a number of directors who work with us regularly, but they still have gaps of a few weeks or months between each batch, during which they go off and direct other programmes such as *Casualty* or *The Bill*. Some of them have been coming and going ever since we started. The ones we like best are the ones who keep the atmosphere light and don't panic if things start to run a little behind schedule.

At rehearsals we are working with the director, the production manager, who works out what we are supposed to be doing and issues the instructions to us on the floor once the director has disappeared into his control box, and the assistant floor manager, who works out our calls and timings.

The next stage for the studio material is the 'tech run' for the camera crew, the sound people, props people, costume and make-up designers, and for the lighting directors to work out where they are going to put the cameras and lights. With outside material we just shoot it on the lot after a couple of rehearsals because the director will have sat down in advance with the technical people to work out what they are all going to be doing. The lot is a series of fibreglass building fronts all constructed round the square in the middle, which is planted up with trees and shrubs as it would be in real life. Occasionally we go on location if we have to include scenes such as the exterior of a hospital (we usually use a BBC building for that) or to somewhere more exotic like Paris. During the tech run we do all the scenes in the order in which they will be filmed, which is planned to find the easiest way for the cameras to move about from one scene to another.

Next comes the 'producer's run' and we go through it all again with the producer, writer and script editor watching. This time we do the scenes in the order they appear in the script so that they can see that the story is panning out and flowing properly, but without the exterior shots, which have already been filmed by then. At this stage they can tell if the episode is too long or too short and can make the necessary adjustments, cutting something or writing new scenes.

Now that we film three episodes a week they try to ensure that the actors get reasonable breaks, which means carefully working out which scenes to do on which days. We always get one day off a week, and if everything works out well we might get two. The producers tell us when we can take our holidays, although they sometimes change their minds as the stories develop.

The main sets like the pub, the café and the Fowlers' house can't be moved easily, so they stay set up all the time. Some of the simpler ones like Phil and Kathy's flat can easily be moved around and these scenes are sometimes shot on a Saturday to alleviate the pressure on the studio during the week. We are contracted to do a certain number of episodes a year, but there is no telling how much work any one of us will have in each episode – it could be anything from a couple of scenes to fourteen, depending on the way the storylines develop. But even if you don't have much to do one particular week you still have to hang round all day waiting for them to finish other people's scenes and get to yours.

★   ★   ★

I was very keyed up and nervous in the early days of the show. In fact the others nicknamed me 'Spewy Huey', because I kept throwing up. When I went in on a Monday morning Wendy Richard would ask, 'Thrown up anywhere nice this weekend, then, Gill?'

There was one particularly embarrassing incident when an old friend of mine called John rang and asked me out for the evening. It was lovely to hear from him and he said as we hadn't seen each other for so long he'd hire a car and we'd do it properly. I had never been in a limousine before and I couldn't believe how luxurious it was, with carpet everywhere. We went for some drinks with friends and then got back in the car to go to a well-known restaurant in the West End. As we cruised through the streets I began to feel a bit unwell. I turned to John to say I thought I was going to be sick and as I spoke my mouth seemed to turn into a fire hydrant and I just shot water all over the interior of the car.

'We'd better get you something to eat quick,' John said and piled me into the restaurant in double time. 'Don't worry about the menu,' he said to the waiter, 'just bring us Châteaubriand for two.'

As we waited for the food I said, 'I think I'm going to be sick again.'

'Can you make it to the ladies'?'

'I don't think so,' and with that I grabbed a napkin and held it to my mouth. It filled up with water like a balloon, with me left holding the corners together and wondering what to do next.

'We'd better get you out of here,' John decided.

'What am I going to do with this?' I wanted to know. 'If they see me going out with it they'll think I'm nicking the cutlery.'

'Just put it under the table,' he said. So I did and we walked out quickly, cancelling the food as we went. I've always felt guilty about whoever found that napkin.

Pam St Clements (Pat in the show) also used to call me 'Leaky Lou', because I was always having to go to the toilet. When Kathy was part of the Queen Vic darts team we went on location to film the team coming and going from other pubs. We stayed at the Tower Hotel in St Katharine's Dock for a few days and started filming very early in the morning before people were up. One morning we actually had to get a publican out of bed to open up and let me get to a toilet – he wasn't best pleased.

Even after all these years I still get nervous before each take, although it's nothing like as bad as it was when the series first started. Whenever I used to get notes from the directors in the beginning it was always to tell me to slow down because I was gabbling. I always have talked too fast, my mouth galloping ahead of my brain – a 'crackerjack display' as Jack Tinker generously described it – and it's often got me into trouble.

Most of the notes come from the director via the production manager's headphones, but if he wants to put across something more difficult the director will come down from the box to talk to you himself. Usually the production manager says something like, 'Fred says that take was really good but he's just coming out to talk to you.'

'Oh, that good, eh?' is usually my response. 'So good that the director's coming on to the floor.'

It is also the production manager's job to tell us all to shut up when we are chatting too much and annoying the director. This tends to happen most when things are running a bit late and they are worried they aren't going to get the material they need by the end of the day. That is when tempers begin to heat up. It happens most often during the pub scenes. The writers like very long pub scenes which involve all of us sitting around even though we haven't got any lines to say. So we tend to talk about other things. If I'm sitting with someone I'm going to be in the next scene with, for instance, we might be rehearsing our lines in one corner while they are setting up or rehearsing, and several other people may be doing the same thing in other parts of the set. Then you have the lighting technicians shouting instructions across to one another and all sorts of other people like make-up coming and going. It can drive the people in the control box mad. Although the time taken over some of the scenes does get a bit boring sometimes I still get a buzz from going in to work, even now. The most difficult bits are things like party scenes, where you have to keep in the party spirit all day for take after take. It's easy enough at ten in the morning, but by half way through the afternoon you can be starting to flag a bit and it is hard to maintain the right atmosphere. If people ask me what I've been doing and I tell them we were just sitting round in the pub doing a party scene, they think I've had a really easy day of it, but it is actually exhausting and I come home in the evenings fit for nothing except a drink, a bath and bed.

Emotional scenes, where you have to cry to order, are the most exciting, but they can also be very draining. During the making of Kathy's rape scenes I used to come home in the evenings feeling really depressed, infected by the mood of the character and the terrible experiences she was undergoing. It's hard to switch off from that sort of mood.

Unless it's something unusual, like an episode with only three or four actors in and a lot of drama, we don't usually get to see the final product until it is broadcast to the nation. Sometimes I watch the show at home, but often I go for weeks without seeing it. When I do see myself on the screen I become far too self-critical about the way I look and the way I am performing. Whenever I was watching it with Mum and Dad I used to be going, 'Oh, look, look at my face! Oh, that's terrible. Why did I do that? What's happened to my mouth? What did I think I was doing?'

'If you can't sit here quietly,' Dad would say, 'go home and watch it.'

It can be useful to watch your own performance because you can see things you are doing wrong and correct them. When I was in *The Rag Trade* I saw that whenever anyone else was talking I was always nodding my head in agreement. On television every movement, every expression or gesture is exaggerated, and I looked like one of those nodding dogs people have on the back shelves of their cars. Once I had realised what I was doing I was able to force myself to stop.

I remember watching one scene in *EastEnders* in which Nick Cotton was blackmailing Kathy. He came into the pub at the end of the episode and lifted his glass to me in a mocking, threatening toast. The camera then stayed on my angry reaction. Sitting in front of the screen a few weeks later I noticed that I inflated my nose to almost three times its size when I was acting indignant. It was a shock to see and I've tried not to do it again.

There's a joke on the set that Kathy Beale is like an angel of death to the career of any actor who comes in for any sort of emotional relationship with her: divorced by a husband who then left the series; raped by a man who got locked up and left the series; rejecting a daughter who then killed herself. Another romantic interest went a bit barmy, dressing her like his wife and leaving the series, while another man she met got stabbed to death . . . the list seems endless. When the news got out that Kathy was going to start going out with Steve McFadden's character, Phil, Adam, who plays Kathy's son Ian, kept teasing him that he must be about be written out: 'Romantic interest with Kathy! Contract up, is it, mate?'

Even when the series started showing I still didn't really understand how big it was becoming. We all knew that audiences were up to twenty million for some episodes, but it is hard to relate that to the work you are doing day in and day out in the studio. At some time or another virtually everyone in the country must have seen me as Kathy, and around a third of them watch with some regularity. It is almost impossible to imagine such statistics. The media talk about us as 'stars', but we all know that we aren't real stars. If the series ended or we were written out we would be forgotten within a few months. I remember once Douglas Fairbanks came up to the studio to visit one of the buildings which was named Fairbanks House. I was dying to meet him and when I heard that he was about to leave I went running through the corridors, desperate not to miss him. He was just climbing into his limousine as I emerged, red-faced and panting. 'Stop,' I shouted. 'Please, can I just say hello?' He must have wondered how such a demented woman had managed to get into the studio, but he was very gracious and the BBC photographer with him asked if he could take our picture. I felt that I had met someone important, someone from the magical world of the movies which I had been watching all my life, which is what real stardom is all about.

We originally had eighteen-month contracts, at the end of which management were talking about switching us to two-year contracts. After we had been doing the series for eighteen months a group of us were chatting about what we would do if they didn't renew our options.

Anita was saying, 'I don't know if I want to go on for another two years. I think I'd like to go back to the theatre.'

Letitia felt the same: 'I wouldn't mind going back to the theatre or picking up my dancing.' They were all joining in and then someone asked me what I thought I would do.

'I don't know,' I said, 'I think I've lost my speed.'

They all sat and looked at me as if to say, 'What?'

'I think I'll have to go to a night course to get my typing speed up again if I'm going to go back to my job.'

'Do you really think you are going to go back to a secretarial job after this?' they asked, amazed at the idea.

'Well, I always have done. I've never been a full-time actor, it depends what Anna Scher can get for me.'

It seemed like the most normal thing in the world for me to say and it was only when I saw their reactions, a mixture of disbelief and hilarity, that I realised my life really had changed once and for all. There was no going back.

Now that I was finally committed to being a full-time actress I thought I had better do something about changing agencies, since I was getting much too old to be on Anna's books. First I went to an agent called John Mahoney, who was really nice, but he represented Wendy Richard and we were often both up for the same jobs, so I thought I had better try someone else. Several people had mentioned Sara Randall, saying how good she would be for me, including Chris Biggins and Leslie Grantham, who was also with her. Sara and I hit it off immediately and I moved to her in the hope that my career would really take off and I might just become famous. I kept forgetting that I was famous already.

7

Getting into the Papers

When *EastEnders* was launched the BBC arranged a lot of interviews and big press conferences. It was all a bit daunting, but quite fun. Whenever they asked me to do an interview about the show I was happy to, which is how I met a journalist called Stuart White from the *News of the World*. The interview went along nicely and then at the end he asked me if anything in my life had ever upset me?

Had I been trained by the BBC publicity department I would have known to say 'No', but I didn't.

'Have you ever been in hospital?' he continued casually.

'No . . . oh, I tell a lie, I did go to hospital once, just before I started *EastEnders*. I had a lump in my breast and I had to have it taken out.' I thought no more about it until I saw the headline a few days later: 'I thought I was going to die with cancer – so I prayed, please God . . .'

My first thought when I read this was how embarrassing it was: I felt that people who really had got cancer were going to be reading it and thinking, all she had was a little lump which wasn't even malignant and she's making all this fuss about it. I hated that they would all assume I had just done it for the publicity, when all I thought I was talking about was my job in *EastEnders* and how I got the part. In fact, finding the lump, as any woman can imagine, was very frightening, but I was lucky and, as ever, my family was wonderfully supportive.

I should have learnt my lesson from that article and from then on I should have known never to mention personal details to reporters unless I wanted to see them blown up out of all proportion. I did become a little more cautious, but I still found it almost impossible to stop myself chatting on to a journalist I liked – and most of them were very good at being likeable. In all honesty I have to admit I find it impossible to stop myself chatting to everyone. If a check-out girl in the supermarket asks me how I am she's likely to get my whole life story before I've finished packing up the shopping.

When the *News of the World* magazine, *Sunday*, wanted to interview me with Debbie and Kim, I thought at least there would be safety in numbers. Imagine my horror when the magazine appeared with a picture of me on the cover and a picture of my cousin Paul inset with the title 'Exclusive. IRA Bomb Killed Our Paul – EastEnder Gillian Taylforth reveals her family tragedy.' We had fallen for exactly the same trick. The reporter had won our confidence and asked us if there had been any tragedies in our family. Without thinking, we told her about our cousin Paul, expecting the story to appear in context, if at all. Paul was the only civilian to be killed in the Guildford bombings. He had gone to Guildford to meet his girlfriend, who was a WRAC, and they were having a joint birthday party in a pub. The bomb was actually under Paul's chair. I was sixteen at the time and it was the first tragedy I had ever had to cope with personally. I can still remember the look on Dad's face when he heard the news over the phone. When he hung up he smashed his fist against the wall, desperately trying not to cry in front of us. Paul had been his widowed sister's son and he had been very close to us, popping in and out of the flat all the time.

Inside the magazine the headlines were just as lurid. The whole first page of the article was taken up with descriptions of the tragedy. There was a huge colour picture of us three, grinning happily for the camera, with black and white pictures of Paul and the bomb damage inset. I felt so awful for my aunt. I didn't want her to think we were cashing in on Paul's death just to get publicity for ourselves. I rang her immediately and she was very understanding, but it must have raked up some horrible memories for her. I could see how it had happened, that it was a dramatic story which is what the media always need, but we still felt we had been betrayed.

For every one article that upset us there were many that were lovely. The reporters might get the odd fact wrong or change the sense of what I had said occasionally, but most of the time I was very happy to talk to the press, telling them about my favourite recipe or modelling knitwear or a glamorous evening dress. Yet the articles that were distorted were the ones which lodged in my mind. Other people told me not to be so sensitive and to forget them, because everyone else would – 'Do you remember anything you read in the papers last week?' they would ask me and I would have to admit that I didn't. But somehow that knowledge didn't help. I couldn't bear the thought that people would be given the wrong impression of me, would believe that I had said things which I hadn't said or would think badly of me. Although none of the early articles ever said anything nasty about me personally, I couldn't get the bad ones out of my mind, replaying in my mind a hundred times what I should have said, telling myself over and over again that next time I would be ready for the traps the interviewers set, not allowing myself to be lulled into telling them anything I did not want to see appearing in headlines.

The next shock was to discover that now I had appeared

in the papers a few times, reporters were trying to persuade acquaintances of mine with offers of money to give ever more personal details about me. When the stories appeared they bore little resemblance to the facts as I remembered them. The first taste I had of this was when a story by an ex-boyfriend of mine appeared.

I had met him when he was doing a director's course at college and needed an actress for the day. Anna sent me along for the job. We chatted a lot and he told me about the girl he was living with. I didn't see him for some months after that. Then one evening, when *EastEnders* was up and running, I was out having a Chinese meal with a cousin of mine in Islington when I noticed a bloke staring at me across the restaurant. I was sure he looked familiar. When my cousin went out to the toilet the bloke's friend came over.

'Excuse me, my friend thinks he knows you. He said he did a film with you once,' and it turned out to be the chap on the director's course. We joined them at their table and were talking away. I asked about his girlfriend.

'We're not doing too well,' he said.

'Oh, no, I'm sorry to hear that.'

'Actually she's away at the moment with another boyfriend of hers. We're still sort of together.'

'Oh, blimey, that's a shame, because you were together quite a while, weren't you?'

At the end of the evening he asked if I would like to go out some time and I said it would be nice to go for a drink, so we made an arrangement. We got on very well, talking about old movies and musicals and we found we liked all the same stuff. We went out for a few months and started a relationship. He still seemed confused about the situation with his previous girlfriend, but I was happy with that. I had just broken up with Tele and I didn't feel ready for a major commitment again so soon. He kept telling me that the other woman was living with him, but going off on holidays with another man. I couldn't understand how he could live like that. Eventually he went to live at his mum and dad's, so I decided he must be telling the truth – like the silly cow I am!

It turned out he'd been married to this girl for two years. She worked at a travel agency, which was why she kept going away.

'You're married?' I couldn't believe it when he finally confessed. 'Why didn't you tell me?'

'I knew you had morals about that sort of thing and you wouldn't have gone out with me if you'd known.'

Some time after that he told his story to the papers, which announced that he had described me as 'desperately insecure and possessive' and had said that my 'violent jealousy' had killed off his love. Soon afterwards his wife's story appeared, with all the headlines making it look as if I had known all along that he was married and had tried to steal him away from her. That was the first time I realised that when your private life gets into the media they can twist it to fit whatever ideas they have about you. It wasn't that this bloke said anything particularly bad about me; he just talked about our break-up and he did say that he knew if he had told me he was married I would never have gone out with him – 'She's an ex-Sunday school teacher,' he was quoted as saying, 'very puritanical.'

But he did say things about my colleagues which upset me a lot. Everyone, when they get home from a hard day's work, is going to have a moan sometimes, and some of those moans will be about people they work with. But when you are going on to your partner about the things that have happened during the day, you don't expect to see those things splashed all over the papers months later, much elaborated on and exaggerated, especially when you've completely forgotten about whatever it was that was upsetting you at the time. I had to go round to everyone at work who was mentioned and apologise to them, which was really horrible. Luckily, they were all very understanding, many of them having had something similar done to them at one time or another. I liked everyone I was working with and was really enjoying myself, so I hated the thought that people would get the wrong idea from what appeared in the papers.

A while after that story broke a girl came to work as an extra on the show and introduced herself to me. She told me that she knew about my ex-boyfriend and his wife and that they were being advised by a publicity man called Max Clifford. I had never heard of him and I didn't take much notice of the name, although in years to come he was to become the most famous person in the country for handling these sorts of stories.

'He's going out with a secretary,' the girl went on, 'and she says she's going to do a story on you.'

'What do you mean?' I didn't understand.

'She says she's going to say that you've been out at a nightclub and you've seen her, gone over and hit her, accusing her of taking your bloke away from you and warning her to leave him alone.'

'I don't even know her.' I was dumbfounded. As it happened the story never appeared and I don't know what the background was. But I do know that it started me thinking about the fact that people could now tell any stories they liked about me and the papers might print them. It was a horrible feeling.

Working in *EastEnders* meant that I no longer had so much time to do the things I liked, like keeping fit, so I started to do Callanetics at home until I found a gym which could fit in with the odd times I was working. I also found that once my face became known I didn't like going to health clubs at busy times of the day with people recognising me. I bought myself a step machine so that I could work out at home, trying to do an hour at a time on it.

Being in the series gave me enough money, for the first time, to do something nice for Mum and Dad; the problem was finding something I could give them that they really wanted that wouldn't embarrass Dad. My aunt and uncle had a caravan down at Dovercourt. Mum and Dad had been going down there a lot and told us how lovely it was. When one of the caravans on the site came up for sale I suggested they should have a look at it; if they liked it, I would buy it for them. Dad was worried about the running costs, but I kept on at him, asking him to let me do something for him while I could. I didn't imagine that I would go on earning well for long and I wanted to enjoy the money while it was there. I talked it over with my brother and sisters first, to make sure none of them objected, and they all offered to help out with the running costs and buying all the things Mum and Dad needed, like second sets of crockery, cutlery and cooking implements, so it became a family venture. Eventually we overcame Dad's reservations and he agreed to let me buy it. We all felt very good about being able to do something for them after all the years that they had been doing things for us. Dad had always refused to get a car, saying that he 'didn't want to put all his eggs in one basket' – meaning us. So whenever they wanted to go to the caravan they had to travel with my aunt and uncle, who went down most weekends.

It was a lovely place and Dad built a garden round the front. At Trader Vic's, the bar at the bottom of the Hilton in Park Lane, they gave away cocktail sticks with little brown figurines on them. I had been collecting them and giving them to Dad. When he built his hedge round this little garden he filled it with these little figures, making them peek out of the bushes and plants at different angles. It looked so funny.

My other big expense was to get myself a new car. I never intended to buy a brand new one, just one that was better than the old bangers I had had up to then. When I saw the white Nova convertible in the showroom, however, I just had to have it and bought it on HP. Although the idea of having a soft top appealed to me, I never actually had the nerve to put the roof down. I thought people would recognise me and think I was being a right flash cow. I gave Sue Tully a lift to work in it one boiling day in the middle of a heat wave.

'Let's put the roof down,' she suggested.

'Oh, no.' I tried to talk her out of it, but she was adamant and I could see that I was being silly. We put it down and set off for work, but I hated every moment of it, certain that everyone we passed was staring at us.

Although I was earning more money than I had ever had before, it was never anything like the amounts that were reported in the papers. Journalists always seem to assume that if you appear on television all the time you must be earning a fortune – perhaps they are confusing us with people like Joan Collins who appear in the big American soap operas which are sold all over the world. I admit that it is good money, but the job brings a lot of other expenses with it. Because of the tax and VAT we have to hire people like accountants to look after everything; because we are working all hours of the day and night, our home lives can be very disrupted; and once we have become public faces we can't do things like just hop on a bus to go into town, or pop down to the local doctor's surgery when we aren't feeling well – not unless we want to have people coming up to us all the time. All this means that we have to pay for our privacy.

Most of the time it's really nice to have people come up and chat and ask for autographs, and most of them are really friendly, but others seem to think they have a right to pin you in a corner and say whatever they want, which can make you feel a bit trapped in any confined space. Quite often they just want to chat about what is happening to the characters in the series, which is great, but there are times when everyone wants to be private.

I have to admit that I am not very good with money. I have very little idea what I am actually earning, leaving everything to my agent and living on what she gives me. I've also been a sucker for every financial services salesman who has knocked on the door. They tell me I should have this pension scheme and that endowment and I get all enthusiastic – 'I'll have some of that, and some of that . . .' – without having much idea what I am buying or why. The other actors in the firm can't believe how divvy I am about it all. Adam Woodyatt sits me down occasionally and tries to explain exactly what we are earning and why and what I should be doing with it. I keep nodding to humour him, but he soon gives up, knowing that he's beating his head against a brick wall.

The opportunities are there to earn extra money for things like PAs (personal appearances), which can mean anything from handing out prizes at a sporting event to opening a supermarket. I do a few things like that, but nearly always for charity or for friends, which means I get a nice bunch of flowers and a cup of tea.

Which of us is in most demand with the public depends a great deal on what the writers have decided to do with us and whether the stories we are involved in strike a chord with a section of the population. I've been lucky in that Kath has had a lot of terrific storylines in the past, and will have them again in the future when the moment is right. That's how it works in a long-running series – the focus moves from one family to another, then one of the writers suddenly remembers something from your character's past and you're in the middle of another terrific drama. It means that sometimes you have pages and pages of dialogue to learn and huge emotional scenes to go through with the media analysing everything your character is up to as if it were real life, and at other times you're not much more than an extra for the pub scenes. It's not a problem, it's just a question of swings and roundabouts. I love it when I'm busy and stretched, but I also value the times when I have less to do and I get a few more days off.

Some years ago Dougie Fielding, who was playing a detective in the show, asked a few of us to open a festival in Reading, near where he lives, and to help collect money for charity. The other 'celebrity' there was the Grand National winner West Tip. They took some photographs of us round West Tip and then a photographer asked if one of us would get on the horse. None of us was sure that it would be allowed but I said I would love to if it was okay. The stable boy said it was fine and helped me up. Once I was in the saddle West Tip was a bit restless and obviously not happy to have me there, so I dismounted. The photographers kept snapping away and the next thing I knew I was in the papers having been 'dumped' by the horse. My agent received a furious letter from the trainers saying that I had acted irresponsibly and threatening all sorts of action. In fact nothing came of it, but a few days later I saw my brother Ronnie.

'Now you really are a star in my eyes, Gilly,' he said.

'Why's that, Ronnie?' I wanted to know.

'Because you were on the front page of *Sporting Life*.'

8

The Rape Scene

Peter Dean, who played my husband Pete in the series, was a really lovely man when we first started working together. From the beginning he made me feel completely at home working with him. He was always funny and joking and made acting as his wife very easy. But after a few months he started to seem a little bit paranoid about certain things. To start with I thought he was just mucking about, complaining about people upstaging him all the time and telling the others what to do, then I realised that he was serious. He gradually appeared to think that everyone was out to ruin his performances and that we all hated him.

One day Peter and I were doing a scene where we had to kiss and it seemed to me that it was getting a bit too realistic. I felt very uncomfortable, but didn't mention it to anyone because I was sure he would just say, 'I was only kissing her, it's in the script.' So I stayed quiet.

'You're married, aren't you?' I said to him soon afterwards, hoping I was making it clear that I didn't want things to continue in the same vein any longer. I had met his wife Jean and got on with her well. She used to work as an extra on the series sometimes. He didn't seem to understand.

More and more often he was saying things to me that I didn't think were right and I began to feel intimidated. I didn't tell anyone about it because I couldn't think how to explain it without sounding as if I was making it up and being paranoid myself. The whole notion that he might find me attractive took me completely by surprise because I never think of myself as the sort of woman that men will find sexy. Letitia tried to teach me how to pout once, but I just looked like Worzel Gummidge. I still think of myself as a tomboy, just as I did when I was a kid, and then there's my voice (Lee Marvin crossed with Arthur Mullard). People tell me that lots of men find these sorts of things attractive, but with an accent like mine? I never dress provocatively, mainly because I don't like my figure. In fact whenever I do dress up a bit for a party at work people are often surprised to find that I'm not actually that big, because I'm usually slopping around in baggy clothes.

I have very conservative taste in clothes, and I don't have much time to go shopping for them anyway. I don't go down to the West End much because I don't know which shops to go to and whenever I do go I find they are all carrying the same thing, whatever happens to be fashionable that week. If I need an outfit I usually go to one of the shops which I know really well, like Lobita's in Muswell Hill or Clusaz, which is near Mum's flat. More often than not I get my everyday jumpers, jeans, denim shirts and shoes from Freeman's or Next catalogues to save having to use up my days off shopping. I keep myself fit and I try to look after things like my skin and hair, but overall I don't expect men to get that excited about my appearance. I do like it when we all get dressed up for a party and everyone is complimenting one another on the way they look, but I always expect men to treat me as just one of their mates who happens to be a woman and that's how it usually is. People tell me that I am too friendly with men, that they interpret it as flirting and that is why I get into trouble so often. But I want to be friendly to everyone and I don't know any other way to do it.

In the end I had to accept that, unlikely as it might seem, Peter appeared to be keen on me and I didn't like the idea at all. When we had to do kissing or touching scenes on the screen I would dread them, fearing that he might overstep the mark but that I wouldn't be able to say anything because it was 'in the script'. Eventually I went to Julia Smith and asked her to do something to help me, telling her I wanted the kissing scenes cut.

'You know Pete,' she tried to calm me, 'he's very insecure.'

I couldn't get her to understand how bad I felt about it all. It seemed to me that Peter was the blue-eyed boy of the series who could do no wrong in anyone's eyes. There was one scene where he was supposed to be lying on top of me on the sofa when Ian, Kathy's son, walked in. When I saw this scene in the script I became very upset. I went to Mum and Dad in tears, asking what I should do.

'You've got to do something,' Dad said, 'you can't go on like this.' I knew he was right, but I didn't think there was any point going back to Julia, so I talked to the director. She changed the scene so that we were standing up talking and were just going to the couch when Ian came in, but the way the scene actually turned out still made me extremely uncomfortable. I felt miserable, but still I didn't think there was anything I could say without being branded as hysterical because we were 'only acting'.

Someone was putting around rumours that I was having affairs with a couple of men in the cast and eventually I confronted Peter with it. He said he didn't know what I was talking about. I was becoming desperate, not knowing what to do. I didn't feel there was anyone I could turn to to help me.

What I didn't know was that other people were beginning to notice what was going on, and they were beginning to talk about it. The rumours were starting to get to Fleet Street, although no one was doing anything about them – yet.

At that stage, the press were more interested in Leslie Grantham, who had managed to turn his character, Dirty Den, into a household name. He was the first one of us to get very heavy treatment at the hands of the press. It was over an incident years before in Germany, for which he had served a prison sentence. When he realised that the media were on to the story he told us all what had happened.

'I have been inside for it,' he said. 'I've served my time, but if any of you don't want to work with me I'll quite understand, you just need to let me know and I'll decide what to do.'

None of us thought it was anything to do with us. He had taken his punishment and he had come clean with us – there seemed no reason why any of us should reproach him for something which had happened so far in the past. All the time he was on the show I never heard anyone say anything nasty about him regarding the incident, so when the media broke the story we were all behind him completely. I liked Leslie a lot, despite his devil-may-care attitude. I know his self-confidence rubbed some people up the wrong way, but he was only messing about most of the time. I guess he had developed an act to cover up his own insecurities, just like the rest of us.

Once I had been in *EastEnders* for a while I felt confident enough to buy myself a little two-bedroom flat at Belmont Court in Highbury. I loved it. The building had been a nurses' home and had just been converted into flats. The developers had put locks on the sash windows so that you could only open them about six inches at the bottom. One evening I was drawing the curtains and I saw a man crossing the road outside. He staggered a bit and then fell face down. Instead of getting up he stayed down, with his hands in his pockets, and began jerking up and down, banging his face against the tarmac. Blood was spreading across the road. 'My God,' I thought, 'he's having a fit.' I dialled 999 and they answered. 'Ambulance, ambulance,' I screamed, 'there's a man having a fit in the road!'

'Where is he?' she asked.

'He's downstairs,' I answered brightly. I was so flustered I was stuttering.

'Whereabouts?' she asked patiently. I suppose they are trained to deal with hysterics.

'Underneath the window.'

'What's your address?' she persevered.

'Oh, right . . .' I gave her the address and hung up, getting ready to run downstairs and help. But as I looked out of the window again I saw one of those invalid transporters drawing up. The driver and his mate were getting out to help. I panicked that they might take him away before the proper ambulance arrived. I banged on the window, but couldn't make them hear. I bent down to shout through the crack at the bottom of the window, pushing my face as far through the gap as I could, 'I've called an ambulance, please don't move him!' This made them look up, but because I was bent double they couldn't see me, so I had to jump up and down pointing to myself and then bend down again to repeat my shouted message.

I realised that I couldn't communicate from there and rushed out to them. They looked a bit puzzled by the arrival of this over-excited woman on the scene and by this time the chap had been lifted on to a wall and was having a cigarette, his face still covered in blood.

'What happened?' they asked me.

'He had a fit,' I explained.

'No, Oi never,' he said in a thick Irish accent. 'Oi've never had a fit in me life.'

At that moment the ambulance arrived and I waved them down frantically. They got out and asked what was happening. The Irishman continued to deny he had ever had a fit. I was beside myself. 'He did, he did,' I shouted indignantly, 'he was going up and down like this.' I proceeded to give a demonstration like some demented chicken.

'It's all right, madam,' they tried to calm me, 'people who have fits often don't remember them.' They turned to him. 'We'd better take you into the hospital.'

'And how am Oi supposed to get back?' he wanted to know.

Fortunately a young man drew up in a car and said he had also seen the fit; he offered to drive the man up to his local doctor, so I was able to go back to my flat confident that my story had been believed.

When people ask me about acting techniques and tips I never know what to say to them. Some actors that I know become very worried about what is motivating their characters, what their backgrounds and feelings are. I've never really been into all that. I'll stand up and say something to the director if I think the writers have given my character a line or an action which I don't think is right, but I don't get intense about it. Usually we are working under such pressure we haven't got time for too much introspection, so when they tell me we are taking some 'poetic licence' I tend to accept it, where other actors would turn it into more of an issue.

Early on in my career.

Me and Debbie.

Disguised as Florrie from Andy Capp, for a fancy-dress contest.

Aged about seven.

With Janice and a couple of monkeys on a day out at Southend.

Me and Debbie trying to look like Freeman's catalogue models.

St Trinian's outing: Kimmie, me and Debbie with Mum in the background and Dad as the spiv.

Aged about sixteen.

Me, Kimmie, Debbie, Ronnie and Janice.

Janice outside the caravan we bought for Mum and Dad, before Dad built the garden.

Tally Taylforth with Mum.

Always the bridesmaid ... Janice, Debbie, Kimmie, me and Jamie.

My on-screen family, the Beales: Ian (Adam Woodyatt), Kathy and Pete (Peter Dean) . . .

. . . and my real-life family: Debbie, Ronnie, Mum, me, Dad, Janice, Kimmie and little Jamie.

The proud parents: Geoff and me with Jessica.

When they wrote in the scene where Kathy was raped by James Wilmott-Brown, played by William Boyde, I could see that it was going to be very intense. I didn't actually do any research, as some of the others might have, such as meeting and talking to people who had been raped, because there wasn't time; one week I was raped, the next week I was getting over it and the week after that we had moved on to a new plot line.

I assumed that the show's researchers and the writer had done their homework before writing the scene and my job was to interpret what they had put down in the script. Afterwards I received a lot of lovely letters from the public, including some from girls who had been raped and felt that we had managed to convey just how they felt at the time. I received one very nice one from a guy whose girlfriend had been raped and who hadn't known how to handle it. He said that having seen the show he was going to talk to her about it and try to find a way to help her. Another young girl said she had been raped and when it was over she had gone round to see an ex-boyfriend for some consolation. She had found him with another bloke and they raped her again. She wanted to know what she should do about telling her mum. I suddenly found that I was in the position of an agony aunt, something I had no training or experience for. I wrote back to her and said that if it was me I would talk to my mum, in fact she would be the first person I'd go to in such a situation. I told her she should do anything rather than be on her own. If she couldn't talk to her mum she should go to the Samaritans or the Citizens' Advice. When I realised that there were going to be a lot of letters like this I decided I was out of my depth. I went to the producers and asked them to pass the mail to someone who was qualified to answer them constructively. I hope they did that and didn't just give them to a secretary to acknowledge.

Filming the actual rape scene wasn't hard because most of the action took place offstage, so that what we showed would not be too strong for an early-evening time slot. The difficult part came when Kathy was persuaded to go to the police and I had to break down while I was telling the story to a policewoman. It was draining and exhausting. But it was the only time that my dad actually commented on my acting other than to take the mickey. We all knew how proud he was of everything we did in life, so we didn't need to get his approval of things, but after watching that scene he did give me a 'Well done', which made me feel very good. They were wonderful scripts and I was very lucky to get the opportunity to do them.

The scenes caused a lot of controversy amongst friends and relatives, who argued about whether Kathy was right to accept Wilmott-Brown's invitation to his flat in the first place. The day after the scene was broadcast my cousin phoned to say she and her husband had just had a row over what Kathy should have done.

Wilmott-Brown was Kathy's boss at the Dagmar pub and she considered him to be a friend. After closing time he invited her up to his flat for a social drink. William Boyde, whom I liked enormously, was very nervous about the whole thing, knowing that his character was going to become very unpopular for hurting Kathy, who was well known for her good works and kindness to everyone. To help justify his actions he had Wilmott-Brown draining a glass every time the camera was on him so that the viewers could see that it was drink which tipped his behaviour over the edge. The tension had been building up between the two characters for some weeks and when we finally got to the filming of the scene I was so nervous I kept bursting into giggles.

Although she was uneasy about it, Kathy accepted the

invitation for a quick drink. They went upstairs and he opened a bottle of champagne, making her more nervous. He then opened his heart to her and asked her to leave Pete and come and live with him. This was the first Kathy had heard about his feelings and she panicked, saying she had to go, standing up and knocking the table over. Wilmott-Brown stood up too, saying, 'You're not going' and pinned her against the wall. We then moved to another scene and then the viewer was outside the Dagmar with Den, who saw a light and looked up, just as Wilmott-Brown came running out, leaving the door open. Den went inside to investigate and found Kathy curled up in a corner with all the damage around her. He picked her up and took her over to Arthur and Pauline's.

The next week Kathy was at the police station with over two pages of monologue, and once the case got to court people wanted to know why she had accepted his invitation to go up to the flat. This is what caused arguments like the one between my cousins. I have this same argument with so many people, and I'm on Kathy's side; what I want to know is why should a woman not be able to accept an invitation to go for a drink from someone she works with or is friends with, just because he is a man? People tell me that I'm naive. 'You must have known he fancied you!' they say, astonished that I have got myself into another awkward situation. Well, no, actually, it didn't occur to me, I just thought we were friends. 'You're too friendly with people,' they say, 'you're too trusting.' I suppose they're right, but it's sad, isn't it?

I was great friends with a guy from our church called George. He joined the army and was stationed in Lincoln, where he met a girl called Sue. George and I used to write to each other all the time and he told me all about Sue. When they eventually came down to London and he introduced me to her she was very stand-offish and cold. During the course of the evening she thawed out and admitted that she hadn't wanted to meet me. 'I was really jealous of you and your letters,' she said, 'and how much George used to talk about you. But now I've met you I'm really relieved, I can see you're not after George.' It hadn't occurred to me for a moment that she would think I might be after her boyfriend. George was just my mate. In the end she became a good friend too. I took her to pick up her wedding dress when they got married and went to her hen night in Lincoln.

Even now, I still don't understand how it is possible to be 'too friendly', which is what people continually tell me I am.

One of the nice things about working in a soap is the relationship you build up with the other cast members, some of whom you get to know very well indeed over the years and can have a great laugh with to alleviate the pressure of the workload. When they decided to record a documentary about the making of *EastEnders* they asked me to narrate it and they hired a crane to take some aerial shots, including one of me arriving on the lot for work. On the sixth floor of the building overlooking the lot is the Green Room, where we all sit and wait to be called to rehearsals and where we learn our lines. There is one big room where most of us are most of the time and then a smaller room where you can go if you want some peace and quiet. When they had finished filming with the crane I asked the director of the documentary if they would take me up on it.

'I don't know,' he looked worried. 'I don't know if we would be covered for insurance.'

'Oh please,' I begged, 'I promise to be good and hold on properly.'

He agreed, and also lent me the big red book which he was carrying all his notes in. I climbed into the crane, all wrapped up in my scarf, and they gradually raised me up to the sixth floor. The rest of the cast, except for Bill Treacher, were in the main Green Room as I mysteriously rose outside the window and started to give the glass a polish with my scarf. Once I had their attention I signalled the crane operator to move me across to the window of the smaller room where Bill was busy learning his lines. The other members of the cast went through one by one and Bill looked very confused as to why there was so much muffled giggling going on around him, until he looked up and saw me hovering in mid-air outside with the red book under my arm.

'You thought you were here to learn your lines,' I shouted in my best Eamonn Andrews accent, 'but tonight, Bill Treacher, this is your life . . .' and I went as if to climb in through the window to get to him.

Bill's face was a picture as the others fell about laughing around him. 'Get down from there before you fall, you daft cow!' he yelled.

9

Nick

When Nick Berry joined the cast of *EastEnders*, he was supposed to be my stepson Wicksy, although as the storylines developed it emerged that he wasn't Pete's son at all. He was, however, roughly the same generation as Kathy's son Ian. In real life Nick is eight years younger than me. He very quickly became a mate during all the hours the two of us were stuck talking behind the vegetable stall during filming. He is a lovely guy and we had a lot in common. For a start we enjoyed all the same old films and stars. I also felt safe with him. Having my ex-boyfriend and his wife telling their stories to the papers had shocked me and made me feel very threatened and insecure, as had my anxieties about Peter's attitude to me. I had completely trusted my previous boyfriend and would never have believed he would do anything like that; I had also really liked Peter to begin with. I was losing faith in my own judgement of other people and Nick helped me to rebuild that trust.

I didn't want to become involved with anyone else who would go rushing off to the newspapers when we broke up, or even before, with details of what I wore to bed or what I said over the breakfast table or why I was impossible to live with. Apart from being an honourable and discreet man, Nick was also in the show with me and was a professional actor. He didn't want to have his private life splashed all over the papers any more than I did. There are some actors who will happily sell their reminiscences after they've been in a successful series, allowing the journalists to put words in their mouths in order to build the stories up and make them controversial. But the ones who are trying to carve out serious careers know that they can't do that or they will have trouble getting jobs next time around, because no one will want to work with them. Acting is a very precarious business and I can quite understand how tempting it must be to give in when you are offered five-figure sums simply for talking to a tabloid reporter for a few hours. Any actor who has just finished a job and has nothing else lined up will be looking for ways to make enough money to stay in the business until the next acting job comes along. But I felt confident that Nick would not be tempted by that any more than I would.

Even though I got on well with Nick as soon as I met him, it was a few months before we started to get to know each other properly. I knew that I liked him, but I thought he just looked on me as someone to have a joke with. As usual I couldn't imagine for a moment that he would fancy me. I invited him to a party and we went out for drinks a few times and had a really good laugh. He was someone who gave me a nice warm feeling when I was around him. Then one evening we went to see *Me and My Girl* and Nick held my hand, which seemed the natural thing for him to do. By the time the show was over and we went for dinner we were arm-in-arm. It all felt very comfortable and romantic and we started a relationship.

Nick was the first man I had ever actually lived with, and even then it was all very casual. He used to stay at my flat and I was much too embarrassed to tell Mum and Dad, although they liked him a lot. Mum kept seeing his clothes around the place and asking me what they were doing there. I would just change the subject. Then I was having some major redecorating done which was going to take a few months and Nick suggested I move in with him while it was happening. We always kept both flats on, which confused the media, who constantly reported that we were breaking up or getting back together again whenever we were spotted taking a piece of furniture in or out of either place. Since we worked together as well as living together, we both felt it was important that we gave each other a little space. Sometimes we would even drive to and from work separately just to have some time to ourselves. At lunchtime Nick would often go off to play table tennis with Tom Watts (who played Lofty), while I had lunch in my dressing room and answered letters or met up with some girlfriends.

We were together for nearly two years and we had a great time, going on nice holidays to places like Key Biscayne in Florida, Barbados and Antigua. In America we were able to go wherever we wanted and not be recognised, which is a weird feeling when you have become used to people staring, whispering or calling out to you wherever you go. Once you get used to it, it is a relief just to be ignored like everyone else, not to be wondering if someone is taking a picture of you eating an ice cream on the beach. Steve McFadden went to America once. 'It was really strange,' he said when he got back. 'Over here I'm supposed to be some sort of sex symbol, over there I'm just another short, bald bloke.' It's always refreshing to meet someone who doesn't know who you are, which is not the same as the people who pretend that they don't know you because they 'never watch soap operas' and within a few minutes are asking you questions about all the other characters.

There were more English people in Barbados, many of them young girls, so a lot of people came up to Nick for autographs. Many of them weren't sure who I was, beyond being his girlfriend and someone else from the programme, which used to put my nose out of joint a bit.

When we travelled in France we could go almost anywhere without being noticed. I love France and have an impractical dream of retiring there one day, should I ever be able to afford to retire. On one holiday we went to Paris, hired a car and drove down to the South of France, stopping off at some lovely hotels along the way. It was an idyllic holiday. One night it was getting a bit late and we hadn't found anywhere to stay when we saw a sign pointing up a dark little country road to a hotel called Château Mount Sally. The hotel loomed out of the evening shadows like a Gothic set for *Psycho* or *The Amityville Horror*. Inside, the décor would have been perfect for Count Dracula's castle. Everything was silent with one man sitting under a single light, watching us come in. I was beginning to giggle nervously. The man led us up a dark, winding staircase while I made jokes to Nick to ease my tension. A medieval axe hung over the door to our room and the bed was straight from the land of the vampires with twisted head and foot boards. The bathroom was like something out of *One Flew Over the Cuckoo's Nest* and the huge, square, enamel bath had a seat in it.

'I'm not getting in that,' I insisted, 'it looks like a torture chamber. I'm bathing in the sink.'

'Don't be ridiculous.' Nick was laughing.

'The moment you get in there they'll turn the electric current on,' I told him. 'See that tap?' He nodded. 'That's acid.'

The whole place was silent and empty as we made our way out to find somewhere to eat. On the way through reception we found two huge wooden doors supposedly leading to a disco. I peered in through the windows in the doors, but there was nothing inside. Once we got into a friendly local restaurant and I'd had a couple of glasses of wine to calm my fears, I began to wonder if Château Mount Sally actually existed or if we'd dreamed the whole thing. By the time we came out of the restaurant it was raining. We drove back to the hotel and went straight up to our room.

'Any minute now,' I said, 'there's going to be a thunderstorm. There has to be.'

At just that moment there was a huge crash of thunder, sending me hysterical. 'The lights are going to go next!' I shrieked, and sure enough they did, leaving us groping around in complete blackness, me screaming my head off and Nick rummaging around for the phone. When he did find it the line was dead.

'If this was a film,' I said, 'we'd be going to find a way out with a pathetic little torch. I'm telling you, Nick, there's no way I'm leaving this room.'

The phone came on first and Nick rang down to tell them about the lights. The man from downstairs brought us up some candles. Beside the bed there were two little cupboard doors. Nick went to open one and I shouted at him to stop, sure that if he did the wall would turn round and we'd end up on the other side, never to be seen again.

I didn't sleep a wink that night and in the middle of the night we heard the steady beat of a disco somewhere in the bowels of the building. 'It's the living dead having a night out,' I whimpered, pulling the sheets over my head and imagining a room full of bopping zombies. Nick was half laughing and half exasperated, trying to get some sleep while I jabbered on. The next morning the place was empty and silent as the grave once more and we left with relief. As we drove off I half expected to look back and see that Château Mount Sally had disappeared like a nightmare in the daylight, only there for a day like something out of *Brigadoon*.

I always felt a bit insecure about the age difference between Nick and me. I really liked him, but I knew that as we grew older this would become more of a problem. After we had been going out for a while Nick's career really started to take off. He had a record in the charts and was appearing on programmes like *Top of the Pops*. I was really proud of him. He always said that he didn't have much of a voice, but I liked his album. All the young girls were after him. If we just went down to the local supermarket girls would come up and kiss him while glaring furiously at me. I did find it funny to start with, partly because he looked so embarrassed whenever it happened, but gradually it started to get to me. I'm a bit of a possessive person anyway, and I found it hard to handle when he received sacks of fan mail, full of letters from women declaring undying love. When we went out to clubs and other public places I would be pushed out of the way by these girls. On one occasion I was even burned by cigarettes and so I stopped going to the do's with him. The relationship was getting rather drifty-drifty and I know I became a bit of a nag, because I was so sure he would find someone he preferred to me. I also knew that he was very ambitious and wanted to go to America to make films. I couldn't imagine that I would fit into his lifestyle when that happened. I would love to do films, too, of course – my dream would have been to be the female lead in an adventure like *Raiders of the Lost Ark*, but I can't see it happening now, apart from which I'm not sure I could handle being away from home for so long.

It was at this time that I had the white convertible Vauxhall Nova, but terrible things kept happening to it and someone even suggested it might be fans of Nick's getting back at me. To start with the roof leaked, which I don't suppose

I can really blame them for. Then the window was broken and the cassettes taken, which again seems like a random crime. The next thing that happened, however, was that while the car was parked in the BBC car park an iron bar was heaved over the fence on to the bonnet, doing a lot of damage. This was followed by some charmer cutting the valves off the tyres so that I had to have four new ones, and someone else putting nails under the next set of tyres. (This did happen to a few other people at the time, so perhaps I am being unduly paranoid.) Then the windscreen was smashed and finally the roof was slashed. This, I decided, was where the car and I should part company. I didn't even bother to have the roof repaired; I just took it down to the Vauxhall dealer and asked them to take it away. I ended up swapping it for a little red Nova SR which I loved and which did not attract so much unwanted attention.

Driving home one day I noticed a car in my rear-view mirror which looked familiar. I felt sure I had seen it before. It followed me up to Nick's flat and then on to Mum's place, where it disappeared. I decided that I must be imagining things, but a few minutes after I left Mum's it was back behind me. I phoned the police as soon as I could, but by that time it had disappeared again. A few days later I discovered that Sue Tully had had the same experience, so I guess it must have been a fan wanting to see where we all lived. Incidents like that, however, make you realise just how vulnerable you are to anyone who might decide to give you a hard time.

Nick and I were invited to sell raffle tickets at a charity do, organised at a West End theatre by Martyn Lewis the newscaster, which Princess Diana was going to be attending. We were all in evening dress and lined up to greet the princess in the foyer. I wasn't next to Nick and when I leaned forward to say something to him I noticed that his bow tie was crooked.

I ran along the line, tweaked it straight and ran back to my place. The next day I read in the paper that 'jumpy Gill had to go and adjust his tie to let everyone know she was with him,' which was annoying, but at least it was fun to meet the princess again.

It was the second time I had met her. The first was when she had expressed a desire to come on to the set of *EastEnders*. She turned up on a freezing cold day wearing nothing but a blouse, leather skirt and jacket. She walked around the lot outside for a bit and then came into the Vic to pull a few pints, which she said was something she had always wanted to do.

'I can't believe you're not cold from walking around out there,' I said conversationally. 'We all get freezing.'

'This,' she said, undoing a button on her blouse, 'is the secret: Damart!' and she revealed a little piece of thermal vest. She was just as beautiful in the flesh as she is in photographs.

Nick's and my life together was much more ordinary than anyone reading the papers would ever believe; mostly we used to go out to restaurants together or have friends round to one or other of our flats. When his single 'Every Loser Wins' got to Number One, I threw a little surprise party for him at the flat, sending him out on an errand while I set everything up and the people arrived. I had a cake made in the shape of a disc. I think he was chuffed by that. Every Sunday Nick used to go off to play football with his mates. He was in a football team that Tom Watts had started and Max Clifford, the publicist, also became involved with. As soon as I heard that name I was wary, remembering what I had heard about his involvement with my ex-boyfriend when he was telling his story. Max would get the boys to go to different clubs to play and would make sure there were plenty of Page Three models around to attract the photographers to the event.

'Be careful of him, Nick,' I warned. 'He's involved in putting stories into the papers.'

'Don't worry,' he assured me, 'he's just a mate.'

When Nick and I did finally break up a story immediately appeared in the press about how he had ditched me for a Page Three model. Nick was on the phone immediately apologising and promising that it was nothing to do with him, that he had just met the girl once at one of the clubs. I was upset after the break-up anyway, my pride badly bruised, and this story, closely followed by another saying Nick had left me for a sixteen-year-old, made me feel even worse. The stories never seem to die away, in fact some of them grow more fanciful with time. Years after Nick and I broke up I read an article saying that I used to take him to glitzy West End clubs and on exotic Caribbean holidays, as if I was some frustrated old woman with a brainless toyboy.

As I was feeling upset I decided to go and stay with a girlfriend who was living in Cyprus. I booked on to a flight and when I sat down I found that someone I recognised was sitting next to me. It was Stuart White from the *News of the World*.

'Oh, hello, Stuart.' I was really surprised. 'Are you going to Cyprus too?'

'I'm coming out with you,' he said, 'to meet the new man in your life.'

'Who's that, then?' I was puzzled.

'He's called Robert Lee, isn't he?'

Robert was a friend I had been out with in a group two or three times for drinks and meals. I told Stuart this, but he didn't seem worried. He ordered us some drinks and we chatted on. He said he'd heard I'd split with Nick, which was common knowledge by then. Then he said, 'We've heard a few things about you and Peter Dean from people who have left the show.'

'Oh yeah?' I was surprised that he was bringing this old chestnut up again.

I was feeling very low and vulnerable and it was nice to have someone to chat to, especially someone who kept buying drinks and dishing out the sympathy. I began to think of Stuart as a friend. If I had wanted to do a story about Peter I would have done it two years before, it seemed like old news to me, so I wasn't too bothered about talking about it now. Stuart did most of the talking and I was just sort of agreeing with him every so often. It seemed as if he had been told about everything and I didn't bother to deny anything – why should I? But I didn't give him anything new either. He kept disappearing to the toilet and I thought the poor chap had a weak bladder, not realising he was checking on his tape recorder.

We parted at the airport and I felt a bit sorry for him for having had a wasted trip. I had a nice holiday with my friend, which lifted my spirits again. About a week after I got back to England Stuart White turned up on my doorstep. 'We're doing this story about you and Peter Dean tomorrow in the *News of the World*.'

'What story?'

'About him harassing you.'

'I haven't given you any story.'

'No, we already have the story, but would you like to make a comment on it?'

'No.'

'I can offer you £30,000 if you will just make a comment.'

'I don't make my money that way.' I was beginning to shake. I felt angry and flustered. I had thought this incident was all behind me now and I didn't relish having it dragged out again with the unpleasantness which would be bound to follow. Stuart went away for a little while and I rang Nick in a panic and asked for his help. He came round and was there when Stuart returned.

'Why don't you leave her alone?' Nick asked him. 'Don't you think you've done enough to her?'

'I've been told to offer you £35,000,' Stuart said to me, ignoring Nick, 'just to make a comment. We're going to run the story anyway, as an exclusive by you, so you might as well earn something from it.'

'I haven't given you an exclusive story,' I wailed. 'I don't want any money from you.'

'Just make a comment and I'll sort the money out.'

'I don't want it.'

He finally got the message and left. In the early hours of the morning I went out to get a first edition of the paper. I took it round to Mum and Dad's and just sat there sobbing. The story had me claiming that Peter had 'begged' me 'to have sex with him', which he had *never* done. It claimed that I had said he had sent me 'love notes' and even 'tried to grope' me in my dressing room, neither of which he had done. If he had sent me love notes I would have had something to use as evidence to back up my story at the time.

When I went into work on the Monday Peter was going berserk, not surprisingly, and both of us were called up to the producer's office, accompanied by our agents and a publicity person from the BBC.

'What's all this about?' the producer asked.

'I've got no idea,' Peter said, wide-eyed and innocent.

'What do you mean, you've got no idea?' I wanted to know.

I explained how the article had happened and how I had had nothing to do with going to the paper. I then went on to say which parts of the story I did think were correct.

'I don't know what she's talking about,' Peter said at last. 'I've only been friends with Gill and I'm sorry if she's taken it the wrong way.'

I just wanted to get hold of him and strangle him. The producers told us that neither of us was to talk to the press for six weeks, which was fine by me as by now I never wanted to talk to them anyway. Everyone else on the programme was very kind and supportive. The next day there was a big story in the papers with Peter answering back all the accusations from the *News of the World*. On the Wednesday there was a follow-up article in which it said that Peter's mother had been rushed to hospital with a heart attack following all the headlines about her son.

I went back round to Mum and Dad's in tears again. 'Peter's mum's had a heart attack, it's all my fault.'

'Why's it your fault?' Mum wanted to know.

'Because that story appeared after Stuart White talked to me. I must send her some flowers.'

'Don't you send any flowers,' Dad growled. 'If she's ill it's got nothing to do with you. This is just hype from the newspapers. What's the matter with you? Can't you see it's all publicity? They're just using you, Gill.'

'But they told us we mustn't do any publicity,' I protested, 'and if his mum's in hospital . . .'

'Wake up, Gillian!' Dad interrupted me angrily. 'It's just for publicity!'

So I shut up. I was beginning to understand, several years too late, what was going on. The next day the papers were quiet and I thought the whole thing was over. On Friday we were back in with a story about how I had been sent to Coventry by the cast because of all the lies I had told about Peter. I was even accused of taking the £35,000 Stuart had offered.

That day I had to go to the garage to get the tyres changed on the car. While I was waiting a bloke came up to me. 'Hallo,' he said, and then added jokily, 'told any more lies lately, have you, Kath?' I felt the tears welling up inside. If this man believed I might be a liar from what he had read in the papers, how many millions of others felt the same way? I couldn't bear the idea that so many people thought I was that sort of person. I just wanted the ground to open up and swallow me whole.

On Saturday Peter's wife Jean, whom I had always got on really well with, was quoted in another paper under the headline 'Why Has Cruel Gill Told Such Evil Lies?' as saying, among other things, that what I was doing to her was 'the lowest of the low'. It seemed to me that the whole world must see me now as the sort of woman who tries to smash up friends' marriages and falsely accuses men of being in love with her. How could I ever let them know the truth when every time I spoke to a reporter I ran the risk of having my words twisted and sensationalised?

The following Sunday the *News of the World* had a new angle on the story: it was reported that they had found a girl who claimed that Peter had tried to chat her up in a hotel restaurant and get her to go to his room, had told her she looked 'just like Kath' and had talked about 'Kath' all evening. She was quoted as saying, 'It was obvious he was totally obsessed with her. He gave me the impression they were having an affair.' Although I wasn't pleased that the story was being dragged out for yet another week, I did feel relieved that someone out there was backing up my story.

Peter and I continued to work together and he did cool down a lot after that, so that within a few weeks it had slipped into the past as far as everyone else was concerned and both Peter and Jean became very friendly towards me again. But inside I still felt badly bruised by the whole business.

That year I did panto for the first time, playing the Genie of the Ring in *Aladdin*, with Lorraine Chase in the lead, Edmund Hockeridge as the Sultan and Jeffrey Holland, with whom I'd worked in *Hi-de-Hi!*, playing Wishee-Washee. It was in Croydon, which suited me because I never like to travel too far away from my home and my family. Lorraine didn't want to do any interviews, so they asked me to do some and I agreed, thinking that it would all be harmless chat about the show. I did a long interview, all about the show, and at the end they asked me about Nick and the break-up.

I should have said, 'No comment', but even after everything that had happened I still found it really hard not to be open and honest with someone when I was talking to them face to face. I said, 'Oh, I just found the age-gap hard to handle.'

When the paper came out it was headlined 'Why I broke up with Wicksy', and had hardly anything about the show in it. I suppose I should have learned to put on an act during interviews and not to allow the journalists to build up any sort of rapport with me, but that would mean changing my whole personality and I don't see why I should have to do that. I love to talk to people and I love being open and honest. Perhaps Lorraine Chase has the right idea and it is better just to refuse to talk to the press at all, but sometimes that gets you a reputation with the publicity people on shows for being 'difficult' (not, I hasten to add, that Lorraine has that sort of reputation with anyone), and I would hate people to think I felt I was too superior to talk to them.

Lorraine was great fun to work with, a lovely, generous person. I had an important do to go to one evening. I took the dress I wanted to wear down to show her and she kitted me out with her jewellery, gloves and even lent me her perfume to go with it. I loved doing panto, but it really was hard work and I don't think I could ever do it again, certainly not now I've got a baby. You have to do matinées, which means getting there at noon, and then you are there until the end of the evening performance, so you don't get home until nearly midnight. You also have to work all over Christmas, only getting Christmas Day off, which means missing out on a lot of family life. I was so nervous going on stage the first week, because I hadn't done any live work since leaving Anna Scher's. They also got me singing, which wasn't in my contract but I couldn't get out of it. I had to sing 'Baubles, Bangles and Beads', which was one of Dad's favourite songs from *Kismet*; 'I Should Be So Lucky' in a duet with Lorraine; and 'It's Not Where You Start It's Where You Finish', which I sang with the whole company. When Dad heard about it he looked very worried. 'Marge,' he said to Mum, 'she's going to ruin my song.'

The thing that impressed him most was that I was going to be working with Edmund Hockeridge, who was one of his singing heroes. Although I knew the name I have to confess I wasn't too sure who Edmund was, but he was a lovely man, we got on really well and he gave me a tape of his songs for Dad.

At the first rehearsal I had to keep asking them to lower the key until they got down to my Lee Marvin level. We were all wired up with radio microphones and in the first week the technicians kept having to turn my mike up in order to hear me. By the end of the week I was getting a bit more confident and they told me they had had to turn the equipment right down. I was dancing, with boy dancers lifting me up into the air. It was all great fun, living out the fantasies I had developed watching the musicals on television on Wednesday nights with all the family, drinking lemonade and eating sweets.

Performing in front of a live audience gives me a tremendous buzz. I can quite see how stage performers become addicted to it. Imagine what it must feel like to be Frank Sinatra or Barbra Streisand and to be up there in the lights singing, with the orchestra behind you, knowing that you have all those tens of thousands of people eating out of your hand, feeling great waves of applause and love coming at you. It must be the greatest high in the world. Unfortunately you need to be able to sing before you have a chance to enjoy that sort of experience, so I'd better be satisfied with panto in Croydon.

A few years later Peter Dean left *EastEnders* and there followed a number of newspaper articles in which he reportedly claimed that his character's downfall had been plotted in a series of secret storylines; that he knew that people involved in the show had wanted to get rid of him; and that Leslie Grantham, as the pub landlord, had repeatedly ruined his lines by crashing the till drawer and banging glasses on the bar. 'If a doctor told me I had terminal cancer,' he was quoted as saying in one particularly charming piece, 'I'd kill Leslie Grantham tomorrow. That's how much I hate him.' I wasn't excused from this tirade either – but at least I felt I wasn't alone any more on this one.

10

Geoff

I met Geoff Knights in November 1988 in the celebrity bar at Brown's nightclub in Great Queen Street. I was out with Nula Conwell, having a chin-wag, when he and a mate he was with asked us if we would like to have a drink with them. Nula and I have a rule that if men buy us drinks we always buy them one back – otherwise they tend to think they own you for the rest of the evening. I had met his friend before at a football match when I was with Nick. I have to admit I did think Geoff was striking looking, very dark and handsome, but I didn't imagine he would be interested in me beyond having a few drinks and laughs.

When Nula and I were ready to leave, the men asked if we wanted to go for something to eat. I wasn't that bothered, but Nula was hungry and talked me into going along. I remember that I talked a lot about Frank Sinatra because he was due to come to London for a concert. I was saying how wonderful I thought he was and how we always used to hear his music around the house when we were little because of Mum and Dad.

'I know a guy who could get tickets for that,' Geoff said, which put him right up in my estimation. A few days later he rang to say he could get them and invited me out. I thought that was a really kind gesture and accepted the invitiation. We had a good laugh, so I was happy to agree to see him again when he asked. He told me all about himself – he came from Ware, in Hertfordshire, and was from a big family, too, three boys and two girls.

We went to a Chinese restaurant and he asked if I had any particular favourites or would I like him to order for both of us. That sounded impressive. 'This chap knows his way round a menu,' I thought, looking forward to hearing what treats he would order. When the waiter came over Geoff asked for 'menu A for two'.

We were invited to join a birthday party at another table in the restaurant because some of the guests recognised me and it was all very friendly. We were near to where Geoff lived and as we left he said casually, 'I've just got to stop off at my house to pick up something, do you mind?'

It sounded like a typical man's line, but I felt I owed it to him to give him the benefit of the doubt. Oh, well, I thought, if he tries anything I'll just have to smack him down. So we went back, he put the television on and poured me an enormous brandy while he went off to do whatever he had to do. A few minutes later he came back into the room with his stuff.

'You ready, then?' he asked. 'Shall we go?

I was really pleased. I thought it was nice that he hadn't tried anything on. He seemed very in control of the whole evening and that was a lovely, comfortable feeling. Then I thought, what's wrong with me, then? Am I that ugly that he doesn't even want to try it on? He took me back to my flat, gave me a kiss goodnight and off he went. The next day he called to say he was in my area for a football match and asked if he could come round to the flat with a few of his friends afterwards. So I bought in lots of lagers and pizzas in preparation for a party. He turned up on his own at about half past ten, a bit the worse for wear.

'Where are all your mates, then?'

'Oh, I sent them home. I thought it was a bit much, bringing them too.'

'I don't mind, they're more than welcome.'

I got him a lager and it was obvious he wasn't fit to drive, so he spent the night on the couch. By that time he had succeeded in arousing my interest and the following week we started our relationship properly.

One of the things I liked best was that Geoff wasn't an actor. I felt that we stood a chance of keeping our private lives private and separate from work. 'I don't want anything about us to get into the papers,' I told Geoff.

'Why not?' He was puzzled, but it wasn't long before he found out.

True to his word, he got four Sinatra tickets so we could go with Mum and Dad, but when it came to it he admitted he wasn't that keen himself, so he gave his ticket to his mum, Jean, who turned out to be lovely. She and Pete, Geoff's dad, have always been so nice to me and made me feel very welcome in their family.

Geoff is very much a self-made man. He had left home when he was in his teens, having fallen out with his dad in the way teenagers do sometimes. Pete is also a self-made man – he'd created his own building firm – and I think there must have been quite a clash of wills when Geoff was young and eager to prove himself. He went off and bought himself a caravan in the woods for £350 cash; he lived in it for a while, until the weather turned too cold. When he sold it he made a profit and moved on to buying a flat, steadily climbing the property-owning ladder until he ended up buying a lovely six-bedroom bungalow out at Nazeing in Essex, as an investment. It had been a convalescent home which Geoff had driven past and fallen in love with, deciding to turn it into a home. I loved going out there because it was so peaceful. There are fields out the back and a stables opposite with a golf course behind them. It was a beautiful house and he had put a lot into improving it.

Geoff was a successful businessman, a director and part-owner of an office supplies company, but he was still one of the lads, going to the football and keeping his Friday nights free to go out with his mates and have a good time. He had started his career as a roof tiler, a description the press loved to hang on him whenever they got the chance, and then he went into the office equipment business, particularly photocopiers. By the time he sold out, after the Thatcher boom when companies were all re-equipping like mad, he was worth quite a bit of money – I don't think he was ever sure how much. But the press had labelled him 'a tycoon' long before that. They loved it when they could say that he had bought a former girlfriend a '£28,000 Mercedes sports car' within a week of knowing her. And they loved it even more when he took the car back when he broke up with her a while later. He was very flamboyant and the reporters he came into contact with made the most of that.

He does have a fierce temper and he can sometimes be a little too protective of me, but there is another side to him as well. I like being looked after and he certainly does that. He's very considerate and he can be romantic, too, coming home with chocolates and flowers when he's only been out to fill the car up with petrol. That sort of thing goes a long way with someone as soppy as me. I've always believed that the man in my life will ride in on a white charger and when Geoff is on form he gives a good impression of a knight in shining armour. He is a brilliant salesman, and he is often warm and generous, there to help out his friends when they need it. Right from the beginning the press referred to him as a 'playboy', a 'tycoon' and a 'millionaire', just because he was in business and had been out with a few girls in the past, a couple of whom had been Page Three models. This image was fuelled by his love of flash cars, including a Ferrari, a Porsche 911 and a Rolls-Royce. Tabloid journalists love to label people and put them in convenient pigeon-holes. Even now, when all his money is gone, they still refer to him as an 'ex-millionaire'. At one stage he met a boxer called Chris Pyatt who was making a comeback and needed some publicity. I said that I would be happy to be photographed with him if that would help and the pictures duly appeared in the papers. For the next few months the media described Geoff as a 'boxing promoter'. I guess it fitted in with their image of him as occasionally being a bit too quick with his fists and a businessman at the same time.

When the press found out that we were going out the headlines were laughable. 'Sexy soap star Gillian Taylforth's fallen madly in love with millionaire,' the *Daily Star* announced a few days after Christmas. '*EastEnder* actress Gillian Taylforth was swept off her feet by dish Geoff Knights three months ago. Keeping mum about claims that Gillian is pregnant and a new year wedding is planned, when quizzed about the baby rumours hunky Geoff (33) grinned and said last night, "You'll have to wait and see."' They had a long wait!

I remember once, when my family were all together, looking across the room and seeing Geoff deep in conversation with my dad. I just watched him for a while and I thought, 'Yes, he's really lovely. What a nice man.' I'll always remember that as a special moment.

Geoff's temper has got him into trouble with the police on several occasions. The first incident was when he caught some blokes smashing his car. There was a punch-up and Geoff broke the nose and jaw of one of them – he was given a suspended sentence by the courts. On another occasion a girlfriend of his was knocked over in a street where traffic was prohibited and Geoff damaged the car in his anger. There were two women inside; the driver got three points off her licence for driving without due care and attention and a £50 fine. Geoff was fined several hundred pounds for criminal damage.

During a fracas in a curry house Geoff hit a man and received a custodial sentence of nine months, serving two months in Wormwood Scrubs before coming out for good behaviour. He told me that that experience had made him very determined not to be sent away again. There was one other incident when he was involved in a fight in a pub and was bound over to keep the peace.

Geoff would be the first to admit that he likes to drink, and that in the past he used to become depressed and drink to try to escape. Despite that he still plays football and tries to compensate for the drinking by training hard. One of the side-effects of the drinking, however, is that since 1984 he has suffered from pancreatitis, and has been to hospital five times in all. He describes it as like having a hunger pain all over the lower part of his body which gradually grows worse, with stabbing pains and feelings of nausea. Apparently the pancreas becomes poisoned and inflamed as a result of heavy drinking and if you have a very severe attack it gives up and you can die.

After the first attack the doctors advised him to stop drinking and he managed to give up for a year, but once he started again he was soon back in hospital. The pattern has stayed the same since, although not every attack is so serious that he has to be hospitalised. The pain is always brought on by alcohol and Geoff has to relieve the pressure on his stomach in any way he can. He says it is like a stomach cramp, fizzing and growing inside. It tends to come and go and gives him signs that it is going to erupt. Sometimes it does erupt and sometimes it just fades away. It always worries me when it happens, and I try to persuade Geoff to drink less – I guess you could say I nag him on the subject – but the illness remains a problem.

Right from the start our relationship was volatile, with lots of rows, most of which were forgotten a few hours later. One night we had an argument up at his house and I stormed out to drive home in my little red Nova. At about one in the morning I was driving down a road and another car was coming towards me. The driver suddenly decided to turn right in front of me without any warning. I swerved to miss him and hit a stationary car, pushing it forward into the back of the one in front, and somehow I ended up in front of them all, piled into a tree. Luckily I had my seat belt on, but I still banged my face on the windscreen and my knees on the dashboard. My nose was bleeding, and people gathered round to help me out of the mess of tangled metal. Two girls came up to me.

'Are you all right?' one of them asked. 'Kath!' she shrieked to her friend. 'It's Kath. Come upstairs and have a cup of tea.' It had not been long since the Wilmott-Brown episode and Kathy was being featured heavily in the show.

Still in a state of considerable shock I let them lead me up to their flat where we were met by two enormous black men, both decked out in chains like Mr T from *The A Team*.

'It's Kath,' the girls told them. 'She's smashed her car.'

'Hallo, Kath,' one of the men said. 'Fancy a rape?' he added jokingly.

I did my best to smile.

They then sat me down with a cup of tea and proceeded to grill me about what was going to happen next in the series. One of the girls even got her little girl out of bed to sit on my lap and collect a very shaky autograph. Before long the police arrived and came upstairs to get me. They asked me to come down to their car to answer some questions.

'So you know our Hilary, do you?' one of the policemen said when we got outside.

'No, they just found me and took me in for a cup of tea. Why, who is she?'

'She's the local hooker.'

The police took all my details and called a breakdown van. Looking at the state of my poor little car, everyone was amazed that I had survived. Once everything was sorted out they drove me home and it was only when I saw myself in the mirror that I realised just how bad I felt. I rang Geoff.

'I've had an accident in the car,' I told him.

'My stomach's really playing up,' he complained and went on to tell me about it. I didn't bother to say anything else, just wanting to crawl into bed and sleep. At half past eight the next morning the phone rang. 'Did you say you'd smashed the car?' he wanted to know. At that moment I completely broke down. Mum and Geoff both came tearing round and carted me off to hospital. I was on crutches for a few days and pieces of glass kept appearing in my head, but I knew I was very lucky to be alive. Nothing could be done for the car, so once I felt strong enough I went back to the Vauxhall garage and bought myself another Nova, grey this time.

Part of the softer side of Geoff is his love of animals. When he found a bird with a broken wing, for instance, he built an aviary on the side of his house so that he could nurse it back to health. All sorts of things found their way into that cage, including a fox which he rescued. We are both as bad as each other when it comes to injured animals. We were driving home recently when we saw a rabbit which had been hit and was lying, twitching, by the side of the road. We stopped the car in the road and reversed back to it, with all the traffic piling up behind, hooting and flashing us. Geoff got out to look at it. I was shouting out of the car, 'Bring it home, bring it home,' but he laid it gently down in the grass.

'You can't bring a wild rabbit home,' he said as he got back into the car, 'it just wouldn't work.' I suppose he was right, but I felt so sad for the poor creature.

Another time he arrived home with a pheasant which he had found at the side of the road. 'Look at this,' he said, holding it up to me, 'it's still warm, look at the eyes.' He opened its eyes and they stared out at me. 'What you've got to do, Gill, is hang it for a bit, then it'll taste beautiful.'

'No way.' I wasn't having any of that. This was not my sort of cooking. 'You take that round to someone else to prepare.' I do like some types of cooking, but mainly cakes and fancy things like trifles. I love doing little sandwiches in different shapes and ice creams, but a roast lunch is not my scene. I'm used to buying my chickens from Marks and Spencer's, ready stuffed so I don't have to do any of that business, and with instructions on the packet about what to do with them. On Christmas Day I always go to my family and Geoff goes to his, and then we have our meal together on Boxing Day. One year he came home and told me he'd ordered the turkey from the butcher's. My heart sank – this meant I was going to have to work from scratch, no instructions and a bird full of insides. 'No,' I said as casually as I could, 'don't worry, I'll get it from Marks.'

'No, I've got it now.' He'd only bought an eighteen-pound turkey for him and me, and a ten-pound one for Mum to do for the whole Taylforth family. I swapped them over, but the ten-pounder was still far too big. I went over to Mum and got her to show me everything I had to do, wiping all the insides out with a kitchen roll (wearing a pair of rubber gloves bought specially for the job). Pouring the water into it I was astonished when it came straight out the other end. It just wasn't what I was expecting. I had thought I would be able to fill it up and then empty it out. Mum gave me some ideas about stuffing it, but when I saw the size of the cavity in this bird I couldn't believe how much stuffing I was going to have to get – it was going to take boxes! Then I discovered that you don't have to fill the bird from end to end, that there is a cavity specially for the job.

Mum gave me all the times for what I had to do on the day – nine o'clock do this, nine thirty do that, but I overslept and didn't wake up till ten o'clock. Now I was completely done for. I got straight on the phone in a panic: 'What shall I do, what shall I do?'

'Calm down, Gill,' she said, 'just add an hour on to all the timings.'

'Oh yes.' I hadn't even thought of that. In the end it all worked out all right.

Christmas Day has always been my favourite time. I can't imagine it without my family around me. We used to arrive at Mum and Dad's at half past ten in the morning to open our presents and Dad would make us a snowball with advocaat. We would all help Mum lay the table. I usually rolled up the napkins like boats because I've never been able to master those rose shapes you get in restaurants. Then we would get out of her way by going round to Aunt Shirley's to swap presents. We didn't usually get to eat until about three in the afternoon. The best bit of the meal for me is the pickles; I have to have gherkins, onions, red cabbage, the lot, plus gravy. Mum always puts up her big imitation green tree and covers it with tinsel, silver balls and all the little decorations that we used to have as children. After we've pulled the crackers and had our photos taken in silly hats we all change into tracksuits and slippers and play games like Trivial Pursuit, Blockbusters or Scruples. In the evening we dress up again and the whole family goes off to Auntie Lil and Uncle Bob's party where we play more games like Give Us a Clue and do turns like Kimmie and me singing 'We're a Couple of Swells', Debbie singing 'Summertime' or 'Funny Valentine' and Ronnie doing 'When Your Old Wedding Ring Was New'. Dad used to do anything by Frank Sinatra. Janice prefers to just listen to the rest of us.

I'm well known amongst my friends and family for not being very domesticated. The first time I moved into a flat of my own I bought a fridge-freezer. My uncle Ernie came round to fix up a few things like the washing machine and the oven. I offered him a cup of tea, but the milk had gone off. 'I'll just pop out and get some more,' I said.

'You've got a fridge here, haven't you?' He looked puzzled. 'Why don't you keep the milk in that?'

'Oh, I meant to ask you,' I said, 'while you're up here today could you plumb it in for me?'

'See that plug there?' he said. 'Try pushing that in and turning on the switch.' I felt such a fool, but I was so pleased to have it up and running that I immediately started filling the freezer with stuff. I was out shopping with Mum a few weeks later and I said I would have to buy some bacon.

'I thought you bought some the other week,' Mum said. 'You haven't used all that yet, have you?'

'No, it was in the freezer.'

'Well, what have you done with it?'

'I had to throw it out, Mum, it went past its sell-by date.'

She couldn't believe her ears. 'It's been in the freezer, Gill. It'll last in there for months.'

I'd been throwing stuff away like there was no tomorrow. I think perhaps I stayed at home with Mum a bit too long.

11

Dad Dies

Dad had emphysema for years and towards the end of his life he had to use a wheelchair to get about. He hated being dependent on other people. One of the papers did a story about him being stuck in a wheelchair and how sad that was for me and the family – the usual thing – and I have never seen him so angry. He was such a proud, independent man and he loathed the idea that he was starting to lose control of his own life.

Everything began to become difficult for him. He had to give up his job because he couldn't manage the journey any more, having to get on and off buses. If he just wanted to comb his hair he had to stop to get his breath between each movement, the effort of lifting his arms being too much for him. He and Mum sold the caravan because it became too hard for him to get down there and he worried about looking after it, not to mention the cost of running it. Every time any of the charges went up he would worry that it was too expensive for us, so I said that he should do whatever made him feel happiest.

Towards the end of 1990, just before his sixtieth birthday, it was obvious that he was going downhill very fast, finding breathing increasingly hard, but he still wouldn't give up his cigarettes, saying that if he was going to die anyway he might as well enjoy himself until he went. He also wanted to keep going down the pub for as long as possible and would get poor old Mum to wheel him down there. She would settle him in a corner and then go home. The publican would ring her when Dad was ready to come home and she would walk down to fetch him. If she wheeled him back to the bottom of the stairs he could just manage to get back up to the flat if he took it very slowly and Mum pushed and pulled. He also talked her into going down to the bookmaker's for him. He never put much money on, just enough to make the races more interesting to watch on the telly. Mum hated doing that, she had never been in a bookmaker's before, especially on her own, but he wrote everything down for her so that she just had to push the note and the money across the counter. He asked me to go down for him one weekend, but I told him I wasn't doing his gambling for him.

One Sunday Mum wheeled him down to the pub as usual, but there wasn't room to leave the wheelchair folded up in the corner as she normally did, so she took it back with her to the flats, meaning to bring it back down when he was ready to come home. She left it at the bottom of the stairs, but when she went to get it it had gone. Poor old Dad had to walk all the way home and it nearly did him in, even with Mum supporting him every step of the way. We all felt so angry about the meanness of the person who took that chair. Ronnie went out searching the area in case it had just been some kids having a bit of fun, who might have dumped it on a street corner somewhere, but he didn't find it. The police went out looking too, but it never turned up. Janice took Mum up to the Red Cross and they very kindly lent us one until we could get a replacement from the doctor.

One day Mum and Debbie decided to take Dad down to Southend, taking Janice's little Jamie for a day out as well. Debbie was heavily pregnant with her daughter Georgia at the time and Mum had her work cut out pushing the wheelchair up and down the hills on her own, so all the carrier bags with their picnic lunch and supplies in were stacked around Dad. The poor man couldn't move for bags and coats and the rest. As they were pushing along the front they came to one of those coin machines where you feed in your money and some clown puppets do a little dance for a few minutes. 'Here,' Mum said, 'let's put some money in here for Jamie.' So they set the machine going and just at that moment Jamie's attention was attracted by something else and he ran off down the street. Debbie went lumbering after him, but Mum could see that she couldn't move very fast and so she set off too. They caught up with Jamie and led him back round the corner to where they had left Dad. When they got to him there was practically steam coming out of his ears. Everyone else having gone, he was trapped on his own in the wheelchair, staring at these stupid clowns bouncing up and down, unable to move in any direction because of the carrier bags, looking for all the world like some half-wit enjoying a day out. He was furious with Mum and Debbie for leaving him on his own and all they could do was laugh because he looked so funny. Debbie was so hysterical she nearly broke her waters.

He found eating very hard because he couldn't breathe while he was chewing. For his last Christmas lunch he had Complan with a sprig of holly stuck in it to provide a bit of festive cheer. The doctor suggested that he should drink Guinness to build his strength up, but it was too heavy for him. The publican said that he might prefer Murphys and he seemed to find that much more comfortable. Before long, however, he wasn't able to get down to the pub at all. So Mum used to go down every lunchtime, exchanging his empty glass from the day before for a full one, which the barman would cover with clingfilm so she could carry it safely back up the path to him, getting plenty of jocular comments from passers-by, which caused her no end of embarrassment. He also liked the odd bottle of sweet Spanish wine, horrible-tasting stuff, which he would get Mum to buy for him. He was used to nasty wine because he had taken to brewing his own wine and beer a few years before. When he was at work he used to print his own labels saying things like 'House of Salisbury, Châteauneuf de Taylforth, Brewed Under Protest in Marge's Front Room.'

Mum did used to complain a lot about all the boxes and bottles cluttering up her sitting room, but he took no notice. He seemed to take particular pleasure in sucking up his various brews through their pipes.

It never occurred to me that he would go so young – he had always been there for us and I was completely unprepared to lose him. It was to be the worst thing that has ever happened to me.

Just before the New Year they took him into hospital. He begged them to let him out for New Year's Eve to be with all of us, and they said it was possible. As the time drew closer they changed their minds and said he couldn't. That was one of the very few times I saw him almost crying – he was gutted. 'Right,' he said, 'that's it.' And he lit up a cigarette, right there in the ward.

'Ron . . .' Mum tried to stop him.

'Margaret.' We knew he was angry when he called her that. 'I've sat here all day without a cigarette so that they would let me out to see in the New Year with my kids and now they say no.'

On New Year's Day they let him out, but the cab driver had to carry him up the stairs to the flat, he couldn't possibly have walked. 'That's not like your father,' Mum said as she watched. 'He's giving up the fight.' He had always been such a proud man and this was so humiliating for him.

Twelve days later he was rushed back into hospital. Mum phoned me at six in the morning to tell me and I drove straight over there. He had always been very strict about all of us covering ourselves up at home, never allowing us girls to walk around in underclothes or anything like that, and always putting a shirt on over his vest if one of us came into a room. But now he was sitting in the bed with his pyjama top gaping open, even though it was a mixed ward.

On the Sunday night they asked Mum if she would like to stay, so we guessed they thought he was near the end. When she came out to tell us she was really crying. 'I think he's lost the will now,' she said, 'he's given up.'

He used to have false teeth and would never be seen without them in. But now he asked me to wash them for him in the basin, which he would never have done before. All five of us were there and we made Mum promise to ring us in the night if anything changed.

On the Monday I had to go to work, but I told Mum that if she phoned I wouldn't. There was no call, so when I got in to the studios I called the hospital and my brother was already there. 'Is Dad all right?'

'Yeah, he's fine.'

'Are you sure, do I need to come in?'

'No, he's all right.'

Two hours later I rang back and got the same reply. Mum said he had come to a bit and was chatting again. I went to the head of our production team and explained the situation, asking to be let off one of the run-throughs so that I could get away early.

'I'll ask the producer,' she said.

'No,' I said, feeling very close to the edge, 'let me explain.

My father is ill in hospital. I'm asking out of politeness. What I'm saying is that I will be going. I thought you would automatically have said, "Of course."'

'I do understand, Gillian,' she assured me. 'I'll have a word with the producer but you must do what you feel is right.'

At two o'clock I rang again and was told he was okay, so I did the technical run-through and then drove like a lunatic down to the hospital, terrified that I was going to be too late. When I got there my brother came running down to me.

'When you go in,' he warned, 'you're going to be very upset, because he doesn't look right. Don't cry in front of Mum. If she sees the look on your face she'll know how bad it is.'

'All right.' I nodded and walked into the room. Dad was lying back with his eyes rolled up into his head. I looked at him and I didn't think I was going to be able to hold back the tears. Mum looked up at me and I summoned all the acting skills I had ever learned.

'Hello, Mum, how's it going? Hello, Dad, you all right? You're looking good.'

'He's all right,' she said quietly.

If he doesn't wake up, I thought, I will have missed my chance to say goodbye. For two hours I paced up and down the room, thinking I was going to go mad, trying to will him to wake up and see me. Finally his eyes fluttered open.

'Look, Ron,' I heard Mum say, 'Gilly's here.'

I rushed back to the side of the bed and he gave me a wink. All five of us kids were with him by then, and Dad's sister; then Geoff came down and chatted to him for a while, but Dad didn't have the strength to talk back to us. At one point the nurses sat him up to wipe his mouth out and his top teeth came out. It made me shiver because he didn't look like our dad any more. They made him comfortable on the pillows and put an oxygen mask over his face so that he could breathe more easily.

At about ten o'clock I heard Mum call his name. Then the doctors rushed in and pulled the screens around him. All of us crowded round the bed, each holding on to a bit of him, frightened to let him go.

'Oh no!' Mum let out a scream and started hitting him.

The nurse rushed back and checked him. 'He's still breathing,' she reassured us.

'He's going to wake up in a minute, Mum,' I joked, 'and he's going to get at you for hitting him. Come on, Dad, they wrote you off ten years ago, but you're still here. Just keep breathing.' We were all cheering him on to keep going. After twenty minutes he couldn't struggle on any more. Mum let out a heart-rending scream and we all broke down into tears. A nurse came over.

'Please take the mask off him,' I said and she did. 'Can I kiss him?' She nodded and I kissed him.

Debbie smeared a few drops of brandy on to his lips. 'Go on, Dad,' she said, 'you have your last taste of that.'

We sat with him for about another twenty minutes and when Mum stood up she slumped to the floor. We carried her out to another room and asked for a doctor to be called. When the lady doctor arrived Mum came round, but she kept calling out for Dad.

'I'm really, really sorry Ron died,' the doctor said.

'Thank you,' I replied, 'and for all you've done. The world has lost a wonderful man. He was a lovely father.'

'I know,' she said. 'I can see that by all of you.'

Dad had such an influence on us all. He's the only man who loved me all my life. The only one. And he loved us all like that. He was 'the man'.

12

Carrying On

We were all so proud of Mum and the way she carried on after
Dad died. They had been together since they were childhood
sweethearts, a very traditional married couple. Her job had
been to run the home and the kids and he took care of the
repairs, the painting and decorating and everything outside
the home. If we made any journeys, he did all the organising
and planning. Without him she didn't even know what bus
to get on to come and visit me, but she refused to be beaten
and gradually got her confidence up. You can still tell she
misses him terribly. I had bought him a collection of Frank
Sinatra concert videos for Christmas, but he only ever got
to see two of them. Mum didn't feel able to watch them
for ages, then one day while she was doing the housework,
she put them on and sat down to watch. When she got very
low, if she didn't have any of us with her, she would stroll
up to the market and chat with old friends there, or go to
visit one of her sisters or a neighbour. The wonderful thing
about living in a community like that is that everyone knows
you and you don't have to be lonely, even when you are left
alone as Mum sometimes is these days.

The funeral was a wonderful service down at the local
church and the service was held by Eileen, the curate. She
let us play Dad's favourite Sinatra records. During the service
we played 'That's Life', then, as they were carrying him out,

we played 'Start spreading the news, I'm leaving today . . .'
Kimmie stood up and gave a talk of three or four pages, all
about him. It was so funny and I admired her so much for
doing it. She choked up now and again, but she got through
it; there was no way I could have done that. We were all
beside ourselves with grief. Eileen was wonderful. We had
first got to know her when Janice and Neil were married
and we really admired the way she involved little Jamie in
his mum and dad's wedding, making sure that he never felt
left out and that it was an important day for him too. She
came to the party after the wedding and danced like Tina
Turner. I couldn't believe my eyes.

It took us a while to organise Dad's headstone and it wasn't
ready by the time his birthday came round at the beginning of
February. Mum felt very sad about that because she wanted
somewhere to go to wish him happy birthday. 'Get your
flowers and cards,' Eileen told us, 'and bring them to the
chapel at the side of the church.' We did as she suggested
and she held a little birthday service for him. We're all
really happy that she is going to be ordained; she will make
a brilliant vicar.

We decided that we needed to redo Mum's flat so that it
wouldn't remind her so much of Dad. We got a decorator
friend, Warren, to help and reorganised everything, changing
their old bedroom into a dining room and making her a new
bedroom. She still couldn't get used to sleeping in a double
bed on her own after sharing it with Dad for thirty-nine years.
Most nights she slept sitting up in the front room with the telly
on for company. It's only now, over three years later, that she
has started to sleep in the little single room which we did for
her. Selfishly speaking, of course, it's great for the rest of us
because it means when we go round to stay we can pinch
the double bed, which is so comfortable you never want

to get out of it. The great thing about sleeping round at Mum's is knowing that you're going to be spoiled with a cup of tea and breakfast in bed in the morning. Personally I can't understand her not wanting to sleep in a double bed on her own – I think it's bliss to have all that space to spread yourself out with no one else to get in the way.

A few months after Dad's death I fell pregnant and conceived Jessica. To begin with I couldn't believe it was possible and I sent Geoff out to buy a pregnancy-testing kit. I didn't want to get it myself in case someone recognised me and phoned the papers. Neither of us thought it would come up positive, in fact Geoff bet me £200 that it wouldn't. I was very shocked when it confirmed that I was pregnant, but Geoff was great and promised to stand beside me whatever I chose to do. I knew by then that I wanted the baby.

We decided to take a holiday before I got too big. We went to Disney World in Florida before flying on to Antigua. It was the longest time we had ever spent together and it was fantastic. After going for a long walk one day I started to bleed a little. I immediately panicked, having been told that the risks of miscarriage are greatest in the first three months of pregnancy. I was straight on the phone to Mum back in England, who told me to put my feet up and take things easy. 'But I want to go to the Magic Kingdom,' I protested, but I did what I was told and then we went on to have a very restful time in Antigua.

We decided not to tell anyone except our immediate families for the first three months in case anything went wrong, but I think the proud father must have been unable to resist telling a few of his mates. When we got back from the Caribbean, still carrying our cases, I found some journalists on the doorstep who wanted to know if it was true. I then had to ring round all my friends and family, even though it was the middle of the night, to tell them the news before they read about it in the papers and wondered why I hadn't told them personally.

'Gillian Taylforth is pregnant by millionaire lover, they have secretly agreed to wed,' the papers told me next day.

When I got in to work Sue Tully and Letitia Dean came rushing across the room shrieking and gave me huge hugs, shouting, 'We can't believe it, it's so wonderful!'

I started to feel nauseous in the evenings and went completely off fish. I developed a real craving for crusty bread, pulling out the middle and just eating the crusts stuffed with cheese and pickled onions.

Geoff and I talked a lot about getting married, but I didn't want to force him into it. I didn't want him to be able to turn round in later years and say he only did it because I was pregnant. I have always wanted to get married, but everything has to be right. When I was bridesmaid to Kim in October 1990 it was my ninth time going up the aisle behind somebody else. Mum has been heard to threaten to take out an advert to find me a husband before I'm too old to make the walk under my own steam.

Foolishly – why do I never learn? – I agreed to do an interview with a journalist, and he asked how I thought Dad would have felt about the baby.

'I think he would have been pleased,' I said. 'I was worried at first about the fact that I wasn't married, because I know how my dad would have felt about that. It's weird that I got pregnant three months after he died. Maybe that was stopping me in the past, or maybe having lost so much love I needed to find a way of getting it back again. Anyway, I think he knows about the baby because we always chat to him when we go down to the cemetery and I've told him all about her.' (I was sure it was going to be a girl.)

What an idiot! I was handing it to them on a plate without realising it. We all used to talk about Dad and refer comments to his picture which stood on the television in Mum's living room in a jokey sort of way. That way it felt like he was still a part of the family and not forgotten.

The paper told the story very differently, painting me as a broken-hearted daughter, sitting on the grave for hours talking to my dead father, 'the tragic printer'. They even said that I had taken down scans of the baby to show him, something which simply was not the case. I felt so bad for Mum when I read it, all I could do was apologise to her.

'How dare they do that to you?' she stormed, furious that even Dad's memory wasn't safe from them.

I have to admit that I did take my scan pictures in to work to show off to everyone. 'Oh, it's a boy, then,' one of the guys said.

'What?' I looked at the picture again. 'No, you idiot, that's its leg!'

We received approaches from so many different newspapers for stories about the pregnancy that the publicity people advised me to sign up with one paper so that all the others would have to leave me alone. We chose to go with *Today* and Jane Moore did a monthly report on how I was progressing and what I was feeling like. Every time another journalist came on to me I was able to say, 'Can't talk to you, I've got this contract with *Today*.' It was great.

I loved being pregnant, that feeling that there was something growing inside me, and taking care of myself, eating all the right foods, and drinking Guinness and Mackeson's, which Mum told me about, and of course the excitement that at the end of nine months there was going to be a new baby, something I'd always wanted. I was continuing to work as normal and the costume department was managing to hide my bump with baggy jumpers and cloths hung strategically over my arm like an Italian waiter as I walked around the café in long shot.

When I was about seven months pregnant, my relationship with Geoff was under a lot of strain and we were living in two different homes, sometimes together and sometimes not. One Thursday evening when I was on my own Geoff kept ringing every couple of hours to check that I was all right. The following night I went over to his house to stay for the weekend. He was always out on Friday nights with his mates, so I was settling myself in at about half past eleven when there was a knock at the door. There were two men on the doorstep and one of them put his calling card to the window, showing that they were from a tabloid newspaper.

I opened the door in my dressing gown and poked my head out. 'What is it?'

'We'd like to talk to you about Geoff.'

'What's happened?'

'Do you know he had a girl here last night?'

Trying to keep as calm as I could I said, 'Well, he's a single man, this is his home, he can do what he wants.'

'We've got tapes of telephone conversations and photographs.'

'Let's have a look at them, then.' My heart was in my mouth by this stage, but I kept standing upright somehow. They showed me a transcript of a telephone conversation in which Geoff was talking about me and the pregnancy to some girl. They didn't have the photographs to back it up, so I kept my cool. 'This could be anyone talking.'

'You don't seem very upset,' he said.

'You'd feel happier if you'd managed to get me in tears, would you? I think you had better go now before Geoff gets back, because if he finds out you have been upsetting me in my condition . . .'

'We haven't upset you, have we?' he asked innocently.

I took a deep breath. 'No, no, you haven't upset me at all. Good night.' I closed the door and as they walked away I collapsed on the floor sobbing, my mind racing. Now I understood why Geoff had phoned me every few hours the night before. He had wanted to check I was there. When I had gathered my thoughts a little I called Barry and Lindsey, friends of Geoff's, and told them what had happened. They said they knew nothing about another woman, but Lindsey said she would come over to pick me up and take me to their house, to avoid me having a row with Geoff when he got back late with a few drinks in him. I was reluctant to start with, but I let them talk me into it.

When I got to see Geoff the next day he told me what had happened. His story was that he had got to know the woman through business because she was an office supplies buyer. She was offered a contract by a newspaper to write a story about Geoff, but decided she didn't want to do it. She wanted to tear the contract up in front of Geoff so he would know she was sincere and ended up staying the night at the house because she was too drunk to leave. Geoff swore she slept in another bedroom.

The paper had apparently taped telephone conversations between them and photographed him dropping her off at the station the following morning. How, he asked me, would they have known to have a photographer waiting at the station if it hadn't been a put-up job? On the Saturday morning the woman's story appeared in the paper. One of the claims she made was that she and Geoff had planned to have a baby and that she was very upset that he and I had been discussing the same baby names – Kimberley and Jake, neither of which were names that had crossed my mind. Apparently he had broken off their relationship when he discovered I was pregnant.

Geoff admitted that during the time he thought she was genuinely going to buy office equipment he and his partner had had dinner with her and he had even met her parents after dropping her off at home one evening. She had also had photographs of herself on a Harley Davidson taken at Geoff's house because she had ambitions to become a Page Three model. He had agreed to that when he thought she was a potential customer. A lot of people have told me I'm a mug to accept Geoff's version of the story, but by the time I'd finished listening to them and listening to him I was so confused I didn't know who to believe. As the pregnancy was now getting near to full term we moved in together so that he would be there for me if I needed him, and prepared for as normal a family life as possible.

A few weeks before I had Jessica, Geoff found a Rottweiler bitch wandering around lost. Unable as usual to pass any animal by, he found a bit of string and brought this dog home to the house. We called her Mabel. She was a nice dog and stayed with us over Christmas. Every morning we'd hear a crash in the sitting room as she pinched another chocolate off the tree and knocked it flat. Each day we raised the chocolates higher up the branches, but she just did it again.

About quarter to six one morning I was already awake because the baby was kicking me and I heard a crash. Assuming it was the Christmas tree going over again I clambered out of bed to go and sort it out. As I got to the door I heard shouting outside the bedroom – 'Get that f. . .ing dog out . . .' Wrenching the door open I came face to face with a man on the landing waving his arms about. I assumed he was a burglar, telling me to get rid of the dog! Did he think I was stupid or what?

'Get rid of the dog!'

'No.' Mabel was barking like a star by now. 'Who are you?'

'Just shut up and get that f. . .ing dog on a lead!'

'Who are you?'

I had to ask three or four times before a woman appeared behind him. 'Police,' she shouted. 'I've got a warrant to search the premises.'

About six more policemen then piled in through the front door, a solid oak job which they had knocked right out of the wall, frame and all, ripping the wallpaper as it came down. I felt myself getting breathless. 'What's happening?'

'We're searching the place for drugs,' she told me.

'Drugs? What are you on about?'

She looked at me. 'How many months pregnant are you?'

'About three weeks to go.'

'Don't worry,' she laughed. 'I've got my Brownie Badge for childbirth.'

'I've got to go to the toilet,' I said.

'All right,' she nodded. 'Leave the door open.'

'I'm not leaving the door open with all these men walking by!'

'I'll get a constable to stand outside.'

I was too desperate to go by now to argue. They started searching and I knew they wouldn't find anything, because I've never had anything to do with drugs and I was pretty sure Geoff never had either. Then they brought in a sniffer dog and I had to stand there while I was being sniffed all over. I felt so insulted. They were splitting up into pairs and going into different rooms at once while Geoff went out to the garages with them. Later I was told they weren't allowed to do that in case one of them tried to plant something. At one stage one of them turned to me and said, 'I know there's nothing here. You can tell that as soon as you walk into a place.'

I rang Kim and told her what was happening. 'I'm doing drug busts all the time,' she said. 'You know the moment you walk in the door if you are going to find anything. There's no way you would think that there was anything like that going on at Geoff's house. Get in touch with someone at the police station as soon as they've gone to get an apology.'

By the time they had finished I was so angry I could have screamed. I made them take their shoes off before they started climbing on the beds to reach things on top of the cupboards, trying to control my breathing all the time. 'Would you climb all over the furniture in your boots if this was your house?' I wanted to know.

We never did find out why they had turned up like that, although we did get an apology and they did pay for the damage they had caused. It was the first time I had ever been on the wrong side of the police and I found the experience frightening. For the first time in my life I had doubts about whether they really were the 'good guys' that I had been brought up to believe in. Predictably, the story made the front page of the *People*.

We soon realised that keeping Mabel permanently was not a practical proposition, so we set about finding her a home. With all the fuss we made you would have thought we were putting a child up for adoption. The first people we went to see owned a palatial home and six acres of garden. They already had a dog, for which they wanted a companion. We left saying we would 'have to think about it'. The next couple weren't as grand but they had a lovely home with a big garden, and didn't have a dog, and we decided that they would really love Mabel as we did. So we gave her to them. It was a sad parting.

With all these emotional ups and downs the pregnancy was not going too well. I had had five scans instead of the normal two or three and the baby was very small. The producers wrote me out of *EastEnders* a month before the baby was due, saying Kathy was going off to stay with her brother to recover from a big show-down with Pete Beale and James Wilmott-Brown. I was able to stay away for four months in all. Adam Woodyatt was going into panto a few days before I left; he went off with a cheery 'Tara then, Mum, best of luck.'

Geoff had all sorts of plans for the baby. He kept saying the first thing he was going to do was teach it to swim. He said it so often I began to think I was going to give birth to a blinking dolphin.

The doctors were worrying that the baby wasn't getting enough nutrition. It was also breech and wouldn't turn. My main worry was that before I knew I was pregnant I had had a bad cough and cold, and had been advised to take some medicine with Codeine in it. As soon as I started to read all the mothering books I found out that Codeine was one of the things you should never take during pregnancy, because it could cause a hare lip or cleft palate. I was so worried that something like that would happen and it would all be my fault.

'Because of your age,' they said, 'it would be too dangerous for us to try to turn it. We'll have to do a Caesarean. What date would you like to have it?' I suddenly felt very afraid. I just wanted to stay pregnant for ever.

I went into the Portland Hospital in the West End, which was wonderful. I would have been happy to stay there for a month's holiday. It was all very carefully planned, although the papers claimed I was 'rushed in for an emergency operation'. The night before I went in, I allowed myself a glass of champagne in a restaurant with Geoff. 'This time tomorrow night,' I said, 'we won't ever be able to just go out and have a meal like this again. Our whole lives will have changed.'

I couldn't sleep much that night. I set the alarm for six o'clock but I was up and ready by half past five. I wasn't allowed to eat or drink anything. When we got to the hospital Geoff and Mum ordered a huge breakfast which they proceeded to scoff in front of me. Mind you, I couldn't have eaten anything anyway, I was far too excited.

The doctors offered me a general anaesthetic, but I said I wanted to be awake to know what was going on, so they gave me an epidural to numb me from the chest downwards. I was so nervous I kept chattering, laughing and making jokes, even as they wheeled me into the theatre. Geoff had insisted on coming in with me, even though he isn't too good with injections. They got him all gowned up with a mask, hat, waterproof shoes, the lot. When he saw the size of the needle I thought he was going to pass out, but he managed to stay upright. The epidural took about twenty minutes to work. They put a cage over me so I couldn't watch them cutting me open and the next thing I saw Geoff had the video out and was filming away. The doctor was waving at the camera and introducing his team. When the razor came out I told Geoff to put the camera away.

'Shall I stay up this end then?' Geoff asked, coming up to my head.

'If you'd stayed at this end in the first place I wouldn't be in the trouble I'm in now,' I told him. The doctor laughed and then set to work, giving a running commentary of the things he was cutting through. 'I feel like Mary Poppins,' I said. 'Any minute now the hat stand and lampshade are going to come out.'

'I'm right through to the uterus now,' he said. 'I'm sure there's a baby in here somewhere. I'll have to rummage around.' I only felt a slight tug as they pulled her out. First a foot came out and they told Geoff to look. To my surprise he did and I felt really proud of him for being able to do that without keeling over. As the video recorded the happy event, Jessica Rae Taylforth-Knights was born and passed up to me and I felt happier than I ever had in my life. I had chosen her second name after watching a Charles Boyer film in which he was in love with a woman called Rae but was too honourable ever to betray his wife and family for her. At the end he was dying and the wife let the woman in to see him. As usual I cried buckets when I saw the film and the name really stuck in my mind. Mum had always said that my baby was going to be a girl because she had done that trick of dangling a needle over my stomach on the end of a piece of cotton. Geoff had been convinced it would be a girl too, although everyone else had said it was a boy because I hadn't put on weight all over and my bump had been up front. I loved the idea of having a little girl.

I was so pleased that I had chosen not to be put to sleep. I would hate to have missed those first few minutes with her, to have woken up in the ward hours later, feeling all muzzy, and to have been handed her then. The moment she appeared my bottom lip began trembling and the sobs started. Geoff kept comforting me, saying, 'Well done' with tears in his eyes, it was such an emotional experience. Mum had been waiting upstairs in the room and they called her down. She burst into tears as well the moment she saw us and held Jess while they stitched me up.

The next day the paediatrician came round to do his checks and ran his finger round the inside of Jessica's mouth, declaring that everything was as it should be. I felt a surge of relief. She was so beautiful. I loved breast-feeding, even though I was so tired. It was something that only I could do for her, just between her and me. It was a wonderful feeling. Anyone could change her nappies and bath her, but none of them could feed her like I could. It was so warm and cosy with just Jess and me together. All the family came into the hospital to see her, including Geoff's eighty-four-year-old grandad, Fred. We took a picture of Jess, Geoff, Geoff's dad and grandad, all four generations together. A lot of friends came too, including Wendy Richard armed with a bottle of champagne, Anna Wing and Sue Tully. Steve McFadden rang and asked to come and meet the baby, but by then I was too exhausted to see anyone else. I also got a big bouquet from Peter and Jean Dean. Jean even volunteered her services for babysitting, which I think showed that the hatchet had been well and truly buried.

When I first brought Jessica home I couldn't stop crying, I loved her so much. I was frightened I wouldn't be able to look after her properly and I used to worry if I was away from her for just a few minutes. After a couple of months I had to think about weaning her so that I could go back to work, and she started waking up all through the night. I became exhausted, even falling asleep while I was feeding her one night. I kept having crying fits, I was so tired. I remember sitting with her and weeping in the front room one morning when Geoff couldn't hear me. Jessie looked up and gave me an enormous smile which suddenly made it all worthwhile. Then I started to cry with happiness instead. As soon as I started filling her up on Formula she went back to sleeping. Apart from anything else, breast-feeding gave me a wonderful feeling of having normal-sized boobs. I thought that developing breasts was going to be a real bonus to the whole childbirth experience. Unfortunately they shrank straight back down to their original size once I stopped feeding.

Each new stage was wonderful, until the day when she

wouldn't let me feed her, pushing me away and saying, 'I do it, Mummy, I do it.' I was so upset to think that my little baby had gone. I rang Mum in floods of tears.

When Jess was about four weeks old the people at work invited us both to a seventh anniversary of the programme. When we got there I had to slide into a side room because Jess wanted feeding. Suddenly Adam came in shouting, 'Mum, you've won an Oscar.' When I eventually came out they had a four-foot inflatable Oscar inscribed 'Best Pregnant Actress and Mother'. I was really touched. There were loads of letters and cards – one lady even sent me a fiver to buy Jess a present.

When she was four months old I started leaving her at the crèche at work, feeling terribly guilty and torn. The first few days I walked around on the verge of tears all the time. I used to ring up all through the day for bulletins, but she was always fine. They were so lovely there and Debbie already knew Gwyneth, who ran it. Everything in my life had changed, all my priorities were different. Jessica was now the most important thing in my world. I loved her so much I was afraid I might burst.

13

A Day at the Races

When Jessie was a few months old I found I had a day off from work in June. Our friends Barry and Lindsey had tickets to Ascot and invited Geoff and me to join them. It sounded like a brilliant idea. It would be my first real day out since having Jessie and Mum agreed to look after her for the day. I've never had any qualms about leaving Jessie with Mum because I know they are both having a wonderful time. I was coming down with a bad cold, but I thought that a break would do me good. My voice had nearly gone already and my throat felt sore. After dropping Jessie off we drove to South Mimms Services to meet Barry and Lindsey, having some breakfast while we waited. They left their car in the car park and we all went down to Ascot in Geoff's Range Rover.

We stopped off at a pub which Barry knew and had a bottle of champagne to get us in the mood. The boys had each had a lager before that and Barry didn't drink much more because he was going to be doing the driving. Lindsey and I had Bucks Fizz and something to eat before we set off for the racecourse.

When we got there we bumped into a group of six girls whom we knew and joined up with them for a while. I was beginning to sound very croaky indeed, but I was determined to keep going and enjoy the day as much as possible. We went on to the bar and ordered more champagne. Barry is a serious racegoer and knows what he is doing. Geoff isn't a gambler at all and Lindsey and I were putting two or three pounds on at a time, just for fun. Barry and Geoff wandered off at one point and Barry came back to us on his own.

'Where's Geoff?' I asked him.

'Last time I saw him he was sitting under a tree.'

'What?'

'He's fallen asleep or something, I don't know.'

'Typical,' I muttered, 'too much to drink. His stomach is probably playing him up.' I decided to leave him to sleep it off rather than go and look for him. I felt annoyed with him for drinking so much when he knew the dangers to his health. I didn't want Jessie to lose her father before she was even old enough to know him. I then bumped into an ex-boyfriend of mine and we were chatting away when Geoff came back, slightly the worse for wear and in a very bad temper.

'Going to introduce me to your friend, are you?' he asked sarkily. By the tone of his voice, I could tell he was annoyed. The other chap got the vibes and wandered off.

'What's the matter with you?' I wanted to know.

'I've been ill. My stomach's playing me up again.'

'You shouldn't be drinking so much.' I started nagging as usual. 'You know it has this effect on you.' I had changed to orange juice by this stage because I could see that I was going to end up driving us both home once we'd said goodbye to Barry and Lindsey. Geoff continued to drink through the afternoon and it all came to an end on a rather sour note when we decided to head back to South Mimms, with both of us fed up with the other one.

'Do you want to have something to eat?' Barry asked as we drove along.

'It might calm my stomach down a bit,' Geoff agreed.

So we stopped for a meal. Geoff ordered a half of lager

which he then didn't drink, so I knew that there was something wrong. He picked at his food. The restaurant staff kindly brought me a big tumbler of hot lemon with honey in it for my throat because I sounded so rough. We then drove on to drop Barry and Lindsey off and I took over the driving as we headed home down the A1 towards Highbury. As we waited at a set of lights I looked across and could see that Geoff was very uncomfortable, fiddling with his belt. When we were driving again I heard him groan. 'I knew I shouldn't have tried to eat anything,' he said, 'my stomach is terrible. You'll have to pull over, I'm going to be sick.'

'I told you!' I was off again. 'You won't take any notice, you have to keep drinking . . .'

'Just pull over, girl,' he interrupted and I could tell from his voice that he was serious. I came to a slip road and turned into it, pulling the car up. It was a really dangerous place to stop because all the cars coming off the motorway had to brake suddenly and draw out into the fast lane to get round us, many of them standing on their horns angrily as they went past. Geoff undid his seat-belt, his belt and the top button of his trousers to relieve the pressure.

'Just leave me for a minute,' he said, slumping back and breathing deeply. I began to be more concerned and regretted going on at him. I had been through these attacks with him before, so I knew that sometimes they wore off, but if they continued to worsen he had to be rushed into hospital. I still had my seat-belt on and the engine was running, with the air-conditioning keeping the windows clear. Now that he was settling back I was beginning to panic about our position on the road. When I had pulled up I'd imagined he would be sick quickly and then we could move on, but I could see that we couldn't stay there much longer without running the risk of causing an accident. I was also aware that we should be getting back for Jessie. I had started to miss her badly now that we were on our way back to her. We had only been stopped a few moments, but I was eager to get going again.

'Look,' I leaned over, 'are you going to be all right?'

'Yeah, just give me a moment.'

I sat back in my seat and found a policeman's face at the window beside me. I put the window down to explain what was happening.

'I know what you were doing,' he said.

'What?'

'I saw what you were doing. You were committing an act of gross indecency.'

'What?' I couldn't think what he meant, because we were sitting there fully clothed – what could we possibly have been doing wrong? I turned to Geoff and saw him with his trousers undone and assumed the policeman thought I had had my hand down the front of them. 'You've got to be joking,' I laughed. 'My boyfriend's ill.'

'Just get out of the car, we'll sort it out in court.' There was not a flicker of amusement on the constable's face and I could see that he was not joking. It seemed he actually intended to give us a hard time.

Geoff was in no mood for this sort of thing and he started swearing at the man, falling out of the side of the car as he ranted on. I climbed out and went round with the policeman to help Geoff, anxious to calm him down. If I could just defuse the argument before it went any further, I reasoned, perhaps the man would give us a warning and let us get on our way. I wanted to be with my baby and I wanted to attend to Geoff's illness, I did not want to be standing by the side of the road arguing the toss with a policeman. By the time we got round the car to him, Geoff was leaning over with a pool of bile at his feet.

'Are you all right, Geoff?'

'Yeah, I'm all right.' He waved me away.

'Look,' I pointed the pool of sick out to the policeman, 'you can see he's not well, he's been sick.'

'We'll sort it all out in court,' was all he could say. 'I know what you were doing. I'll have you for gross indecency.' This set Geoff off again on another tirade. 'If you don't stop this behaviour,' the constable warned him, 'I'm going to call for assistance and I'll have you for Section 5 Public Order.'

'What's that, then?' I asked.

'Abusive behaviour to the police.'

'Oh. Come on, Geoff, just calm down.' I tried once again to bring things more under control. 'Listen, he's not well and I've got to get back to pick up my baby from my mum.' But neither of them would let up – the policeman kept saying he was going to have us in court and Geoff kept on arguing with him, until in the end the policeman radioed for assistance.

Four of his colleagues appeared as if from nowhere. They must have been parked just round the corner and they came running across the grass towards us, shouting 'Don't worry, we're coming.' It was like something out of *Bugsy Malone*. The original one took details off me while the others dealt with Geoff. Then they let me go.

'Go home,' Geoff said to me. 'Get Jessie and go home.'

'I don't believe this is happening.' I was dazed and unsure what to do for the best. I did want to go for Jessie, but I didn't want to leave Geoff behind in the state he was in. 'What about you, are you going to be all right?'

'Don't worry about me, girl, I'll be all right.' He seemed to have calmed down now and I climbed into the car.

'This is stupid,' I kept saying. 'He's ill.'

I drove a couple of feet and stopped, climbing out again on to the running board and shouting back, 'You can't do this to us, it's disgusting!'

'Shut your mouth,' one of the coppers snarled, 'or we'll take you in and all.'

'Get home,' Geoff shouted, 'and get the baby.' Now that he was thinking more clearly he was afraid that they might breathalyse me and that I might be over the limit from the champagne I had had in the morning. So I drove away, leaving him behind.

Kelvin (Paul Medford) and me with a Dirty Den coat hanger.

Big Ron, a popular supporting player in the Square.

With Sue Tully on set.

Party time in the dressing room.

With Dad and Mum.

The Dolly Dewdrop Club. *Left:* Linda Davidson, Hilary Nash, Anita Dobson, me, Letitia Dean and Sue Tully.

Getting carried away in a Turkish restaurant.

Mike Reid looking gormless and me in the arms of William Boyde, Kath's on-screen rapist.

Letitia, me and Sue trying to disguise our double chins.

Dad and Mum visit the Square.

Romance in Paris for Kathy and Phil.

In panto with, *left*, Edmund Hockeridge and, *right*, Lorraine Chase.

With Douglas Fairbanks Jnr.

Everyone likes to watch themselves on the monitors.

By the time you see this photo, Kath's marriage to Phil will seem like ancient history, but when the picture was taken the future of the relationship was still up in the air as far as viewers were concerned. The final outcome was being kept somewhat hush-hush, but after we'd shot the wedding scenes I persuaded someone to sneak this polaroid - at the insistence of my publisher!

14

The Nightmare Begins

As I drove, the tears were pouring down my face and my throat was hurting from shouting. What sort of people did they think we were that we would stop on a major slip road for sex? It was just ridiculous. The more I thought about the accusation the more ludicrous it seemed. A few yards from where we had stopped there was a nature reserve where we could easily have pulled up and done anything we wanted. Another fifteen minutes driving and we would have been back at the flat. I was still recovering from a Caesarean birth and was coming down with flu. We had also been rowing and we were hardly at a stage in our relationship where we couldn't control our urges – we had been together for years. Besides any of that, Geoff was throwing up.

I was worried about Geoff and how they would treat him. If they didn't believe that he was ill, would they allow him to see a doctor if the pains got worse? By the time I got to Mum's I was on the verge of collapse. I banged on the door and fell inside when she opened it, sobbing.

'What's happened?' she wanted to know. 'Has there been an accident? Where's Geoff?'

'I'll tell you in a minute, I've got to make a call.'

I went straight to the phone and called the police station. 'Is Geoff Knights there?'

'Who are you?'

'I'm his fiancée, can you tell me what you're keeping him in for?'

'We'll let you know when we decide.'

'Has he seen a doctor?'

'We've offered, but he doesn't want one.'

I started to get upset again and Mum took the phone off me, trying to find out what was going on, but the policeman rang off. I sat down and explained everything to her.

'But what did they think you were doing?' she asked.

'I don't know, Mum. I think he must have thought I had my hand down Geoff's trousers, I can't think what else it can be, but it's ridiculous, you should have seen where we were parked.'

A few hours later Geoff phoned to say they had let him out and he had walked round to my sister Janice's house in Borehamwood.

'What happened?' I wanted to know.

'Oh, I don't know.' He sounded quite relaxed. 'I got a condition or something for Section Five Public Order, being abusive to the police.'

It turned out that this 'condition' was actually a caution, which sounded to me like a warning. While he was at the police station he had discovered that the copper was telling everyone down there that he had caught us having oral sex.

'Oral sex?' I couldn't believe what he was saying. 'I'd have to have a neck like a giraffe the position I was in – or you'd have to be really well endowed.'

'The first copper said that when he arrived you had your head in my lap and you were orally masturbating me. I went bloody mad. I told him to take his uniform off and come outside.'

We assumed that was the last we were going to hear about

the matter. It was infuriating to be falsely accused like that, but it didn't seem as if anything was going to be taken any further. By the time I was back at work two days later I was able to see the funny side of the whole business and when people asked if we'd had a nice time at the races I turned it into a funny story – 'Here, you'll never guess what happened to us on the way home . . .' I remember laughing about it in make-up and telling them what we'd been accused of.

'Who, you of all people?' They thought it was hysterical that anyone would think that I would do anything like that. Mum didn't even know what a 'blow job' was until we all explained it to her. There were quite a few things that came as a surprise to Mum. She used to feel very uncomfortable whenever Colin and Barry, the gay couple in *EastEnders*, embraced on screen. She usually chose that moment to go out to the kitchen to make a cup of tea. Dad did the same when I had to appear in my petticoat once. In fact, the producers had wanted me to appear in bra and pants, but I decided that if I did that Dad might well kill me.

Later in the day I got a message from our publicity department to say that Stuart Higgins from the *Sun* was trying to contact me. I thought it must be something to do with a feature I was doing for their beauty page, so I called him back.

'Oh, Gillian.' He was very solicitous. 'What can I say? We've had the police on to us.'

I was speechless as he quoted me, word for word, what had been written in the police notes. I was spluttering away, unable to believe that he was taking it seriously. In the notebook the policeman had written that he was arresting Geoff for abusive behaviour; the same charge appeared on the sheet which had been filled in at the station, but above that, I was later to discover, squashed in in what looked to me like different handwriting, had been the added charge of outraging public decency. Geoff had signed his name to this accusation.

'I didn't know what I was signing,' Geoff told me later. 'I was drunk, half asleep and my stomach was still hurting. They were pushing bits of paper at me and I thought I was signing to admit the abusive behaviour. I would never have signed if I thought they had put an indecent act down there. Imagine if I ever had to go back inside again, they'd have me down as some sort of pervert.'

I told Stuart Higgins the true story while, unknown to me, he was recording every word.

'Well,' he said at last, 'I don't know, the police story is different.'

That night the *Daily Star* rang as well and the next morning Geoff went out early to get the papers to see if they had used the story. I honestly thought that they would have decided, having heard the truth from me, that it wasn't worth using. I was still that naive, even after all my previous experiences with the press. I should have kept my mouth shut, because in giving my version of events over the phone I had provided them with all these quotes denying everything. If I had kept quiet they would only have had the police information to work with, but I was so disgusted with the whole thing I couldn't keep quiet. The story was all over the front pages – 'TV Kathy's Sex Romp Fury' – everything the police had accused us of, everything I had said to Stuart Higgins on the phone. I felt as dirty and ashamed as if it had been true. I rang Mum and begged her not to read any of it.

'You know I don't take a paper, darling,' she said.

'I know, Mum,' I said, 'but someone will show it to you, and I just don't want you to read these disgusting things about me. If Dad had been here, this would have killed him.' Later editions of the *Sun* withdrew references to oral sex, leaving it just as a 'sex romp', but as far as I was concerned the damage was already done. God only knew how many copies of the paper were already in circulation containing these dreadful accusations.

Most Saturday mornings I would go down to the market with Mum to do my weekly shop, but that morning I told her I didn't think I could face it, knowing what everyone would be saying and thinking.

'Don't you be so bloody stupid,' Mum said. 'You get down here. Everyone round here knows you, they know you wouldn't do something like this.'

I did as she told me and went out with her and Janice. She was quite right, everyone we met was very nice, but I felt awful, just waiting for someone to shout something and imagining what they were saying to one another once I had gone past.

All the family thought that I should do something about it this time. 'When are you going to answer these people back?' Mum wanted to know. 'You can't go on just letting them say whatever they want about you.' We all talked about it and decided that Dad's advice would have been the same – he would have wanted us to fight them and not just to have sat back and let the lies go past. I stayed in on the Sunday and felt just as bad going in to work on Monday; I found myself crying all the time. I phoned my agent Sara.

'I've got to do something about it this time,' I told her. 'I can't take any more, what they are saying about me now is just disgusting. I've got a daughter now, I want to stop the stories at this stage so that she won't have to hear them when she is older. I don't want her to be told in the playground about things her mummy and daddy were supposed to have done in a Range Rover on the A1 years ago.'

'Do you want to go to a solicitor?' Sara asked.

'Yes. If I let it go, what else will they write about me? Perhaps if I make a stand this time they'll leave me alone and next time they'll check that a story about me is true before they use it.'

Yes, I was still that naive.

15

More Stories in the Press

I had a colleague at work – let's call him Mark – who was a good friend. We often used to chat or go out to lunch in a group, gossiping about work. I was invited to a hen night for one of the girls who worked on the production side of the programme. She'd also invited Mark and some of the other blokes. At first I was reluctant to go because Geoff's stomach had been playing him up again and he was in hospital on a drip. I didn't want him to feel he was stuck there while I was out enjoying myself, but he told me not to be silly and to go. I still felt a bit guilty about leaving him on his own, but I'd promised my friend I'd go before Geoff was taken ill, so I was relieved that he didn't mind and went off confident that he was being well looked after. What I didn't know was that soon after I left him in the hospital Geoff got fed up, discharged himself and went home.

It was a good party and we had a lot of laughs. Mark had a driver there and offered me a lift home. When we got there he walked me up to the block from the car and we were laughing about the evening and looking forward to our friend's wedding when the door flew open and Geoff came storming out, got hold of Mark and punched him.

'What's going on?' I shouted, trying to pull him off as neighbours started to appear from the flats to see what was happening. 'You are mad!' I turned on Geoff. 'What are you doing?'

'I didn't know what was going on with you two . . .'

'Don't be stupid, the man was fetching me home.'

Poor Mark stumbled off to the car and I didn't see him at work for a few days, by which time his black eye had developed into something very dramatic and he had a few stitches.

The night before I'd gone back to work Jessica had poked me in the eyeball when I was putting her to bed. She had managed to open up the tear which the mascara brush had made in my cornea all those years before and my eye swelled up as if I had been in a fight, too. I had ended up having to go to Moorfields Eye Hospital. I had to have a pad on my eye, which I was wearing into work that day, so Mark and I looked like a right pair.

'I'm so sorry Mark.' I was horrified to see the damage Geoff had done to him. 'What can I say? Geoff was a bit keyed up because he'd been in hospital for a few days. He obviously thought I'd been out having a good time while he was stuck in there.' Mark was very good about it and said to forget it.

The next day the tabloid reporters were round at the flats, telling us they were going to do a story about the black eyes. I tried to explain what had happened but, as usual, it didn't work. I even showed them that I hadn't got a black eye, it was just red and sore from the torn cornea. On Friday my picture, with the damaged eye, was taking up virtually all the front page. On the Saturday they ran a story with Mark's wife suspecting me of having an affair with her husband and linked the two 'black eyes' together. Mark's wife said some pretty bad things about me, but I later discovered that the reporters had asked her if she knew that Mark and I were together at that very moment, when in fact we were in completely different places, so it was hardly surprising that she sounded off on the subject into their tape recorders. The reporters wound her up into giving them quotes that they could twist around and make a story of. It made me all the more determined to take a stand against the press. It was becoming ridiculous. As far as I was concerned they had used Mark's wife just as they had used me, setting us against each other with innuendoes and suggestions. If they were allowed to keep this up all the men I ever worked with would be frightened to say good morning to me in case the press found out and rang their wives up. I wouldn't be able to go into a pub or a restaurant or a party anywhere if there were any spare men in the room.

I'd already met the solicitor that Sara had found, so I went to him again and he got us an out-of-court settlement from the paper. This seemed promising and I began to feel that we might actually be getting somewhere in our fight back.

The solicitor was a man called William Garnett. 'I know just how you feel about the media,' he told us sympathetically. 'My sister has the same trouble with them.'

'Who's your sister, then?' I asked.

'Virginia Bottomley.'

Since she was constantly in the media at the time for the unpopular work she was doing as Secretary of State for Health, I'm not sure if this bit of news made me feel more or less confident about the direction in which we were heading. William thought we had a good chance of winning against the *Sun*. This feeling was reinforced when we received an offer of a few thousand pounds' compensation from the *Daily Star*. A colleague of William's advised us to refuse the *Daily Star*'s offer at this stage as it would look as if we were trying to hush things up quickly – which was exactly what I wanted to do. I wasn't interested in getting any money, I just wanted an apology for my family and confidence that the papers would never be able to print the story again. Taylforth is my family's name and it means a lot to me. It was my father's name and I felt I owed it to him to clear it. Now that I had Jessica to think about I didn't want to have this story brought up again and again whenever my name was mentioned in the press. The solicitor said, however, that the *Sun* would never back down because they had got the police on their side. We would still have to go to court to fight them, so we might as well wait and then, if we won, maybe go for the *Daily Star* as well. I still think that if we had accepted the *Daily Star*'s offer it might have strengthened our case against the *Sun*, but I was willing to be advised by the experts. He warned us that once the trial started there would be a lot of publicity. This had already dawned on me and I wasn't looking forward to the ordeal, but I couldn't see any way round it apart from just keeping quiet and continuing to let them say whatever they wanted.

'The *Sun* has a QC called George Carman,' William told us. 'He is very good indeed at winning the cases he takes on, so we will need someone just as good to match him in court and I'm afraid we will have to pay for it. We suggest going to a man called Michael Beloff.'

If we had only stopped then everyone probably would have forgotten the story by now, but – despite the expense – I was convinced that I was right to go ahead and fight them. I am still convinced that I was right to do it, but several times I nearly lost my nerve and called the whole thing off, particularly when the bills from the solicitors kept coming in. I sold my flat and handed over everything from my bank account, but I was still so angry I was determined to fight on. One day, when we were at a particularly low ebb, we did waver and enquired what would happen if we withdrew the case now. We were told that we would probably have to pay the *Sun*'s legal costs so far, on top of our own, which would be hundreds of thousands of pounds. It seemed there was no turning back.

Michael Beloff, whom we both liked, said that he thought we could win the case, but asked us to be scrupulously honest with him about anything we had done in the past. He warned us that George Carman was famous for being able to find skeletons in people's cupboards that even they had forgotten were there, and using them to discredit them. Geoff told him all about his past, including the fights and the prison sentence he had had when he was younger. Michael listened and nodded and decided that he could get round that since it was my reputation that we were trying to protect by bringing the case, not Geoff's. He came back to me; had I done anything in the past which George Carman could dig out and use against me? I racked my brain, but I couldn't think of anything. I'd lived at home till I was twenty-seven, for God's sake, I hadn't had that much time to get up to anything. I'd never been near drugs or any of the things which the media like to use against people.

The strain continued to build on Geoff's and my relationship. It had always been very volatile, right from the start. I still wasn't putting pressure on him to marry me, but I did think he needed to be a bit more responsible towards me and Jessica, cutting down on his drinking and nights out with his mates. On the other side he never liked it when I had to put my work in front of something he wanted to do, or when I went out with colleagues on a social basis. He believed that I put *EastEnders* before my relationship with him. In a way I suppose he was right. I am always under a lot of pressure to learn lines and spend long hours on location or at the studio. I am often too exhausted at the end of the day to want to go out, preferring to put Jessica to bed and then flop out myself. I'm not alone in these problems – everyone else in the cast has the same demands on their time and some of them have partners who occasionally find it difficult to take.

At work Adam is always teasing me about getting married and asking Geoff when he's 'going to make an honest woman of my mum?'

Neither of us has been married and we are used to doing what we want. Both of us are strong characters, used to our independence. It's not as if we were a couple in our early twenties. I have a career and Geoff has been looking after himself since he left home at seventeen. We have both become more selfish as we have grown older and it makes it harder for us to live together than it might be for other couples who started when they were younger. I'm very proud of the way Geoff has built up his business and created his own home and I wouldn't want to change him. The newspapers keep painting us as having a relationship like Elizabeth Taylor and Richard Burton, with rows every week. That simply isn't the case. If we'd had even half as many rows as they say, I would have given up on us years ago. We've had our ups and downs, and no doubt we will have many more, just like any other couple, but it's nowhere near the way it's been portrayed. Quite often we've actually been sitting together reading reports in the morning papers about how we have split up. At one time they claimed we were splitting because of the pressures of Geoff's business, with him dashing around so much we hardly saw one another, but most of the time they just keep uncovering girls that he is supposed to have been having affairs with. Although I believe him when he tells me that the stories are set-up jobs – I have after all had experience of that happening to me – I can't help but feel insecure when I keep reading these things and in my lowest moments I start to question whether I am being too trusting, whether everyone else is right and I am being taken for a fool. Geoff is out and about a lot and I have no way of knowing what he is up to when he is away from me. I have to trust him, like millions of other people have to trust their partners when they are apart, but most people don't have to hear endless rumours and accusations about their partners all the time.

One journalist happened to be in a restaurant where Geoff and I were eating one evening and saw me wagging my finger at Geoff during the meal. He then saw me paying the bill. Somehow he managed to drum up a story from that about how I was telling Geoff off for sleeping with other women, but paying to keep him at the same time. The *News of the World* came up with the best headline when they were accusing Geoff of having an affair with someone or other: 'Two gorgeous she cats are battling for the love of hunky millionaire Geoff Knights'. A gorgeous she cat – me? Apparently I said, 'Keep your paws off my man' to the other 'gorgeous she cat'. I can see the funny side of these headlines, but it all seems so sordid and so different from how I see my life being in reality. In the days of the Hollywood studio system actresses were protected from the press by armies of publicity and image-making people. They were also, with a few exceptions, made rich enough to isolate themselves from prying cameras with high walls and security systems. I certainly wouldn't want to live in an ivory tower like that, but I do feel very vulnerable sometimes. I have to do my shopping in the supermarket like everyone else, where anyone can shout abuse at me or start asking personal questions. And if reporters come to the door or ring up I have to deal with their questions myself, on the spot. As a result I sometimes lose my cool and say the wrong things. Then my hasty, unprepared words are blown up into headlines again and the public's impression of what I am like is distorted even further.

The media seem to be able to accuse you of doing whatever they want. As long as they can find someone to make up a story or be quoted denying it they have something to print, and it is only when someone is rich or powerful enough to take them on that they have to back down. I have had most things written about me now, and if I had done half of them I wouldn't be able to walk straight, let alone get to work each morning. They have had me sleeping with men I've never even met. At one stage, when they wanted to show how stressed out I was, a paper quoted a 'friend' as saying I was smoking endless cigarettes, when in reality I've never smoked one in my entire life. People always think that I'm a smoker because of my voice, which does sound as if I'm a three-pack-a-day addict, I admit. I've never had anything to do with drugs either, although I have occasionally been with people who have gone off to have a few 'puffs'. It just doesn't interest me. I like to dance, I like to have a good laugh and I do like the odd glass or two of wine. I daresay on some occasions I have a few more than I should, but that is about as close as I ever get to debauchery. My idea of a good night out is to come home from work, relax in a hot bath with a glass of wine, do myself up a bit, have another glass and then go out with a bunch of mates and dance the night away. People I've been out with have sometimes had trouble getting me off the dance floor when they've been ready to go home, but that's not exactly the sort of stuff front pages are made of.

I was in a very noisy club with Nick Berry once, sitting at the bar. The girl on the other side of Nick asked him something and he shook his head. She then leaned across him to me and shouted, 'Do you want a light?'

'No, thanks,' I said, 'I don't smoke.'

'Do you want a light?' she repeated.

'No.' I mouthed the words for emphasis. 'I don't smoke.'

She asked me a couple more times until I started to get a bit ratty. A little while later I went out to the toilets and the girl followed me. 'I was asking if you wanted to do a line,' she said and I realised she meant cocaine.

'No,' I said indignantly, 'I don't do anything like that.' As I went out I turned back and heard myself adding, 'And I don't smoke, either!'

The everyday grind of working on a series is also a long way from the image which people have if they believe the newspapers and magazines. I always like it if the scriptwriters take Kathy off to a different location just to vary the pace. I think the viewers like to see the characters move about a bit too. When the producers wanted to get Kathy and Phil together they arranged for several of the characters to go on a trip to Paris. There were Grant and Sharon, Kathy and Phil, and Frank and Pat. We all had a great time; it felt like 'real filming' as opposed to the daily routine of the studio and back lot. Phil and Kathy were left on their own during the evening and went to have supper together. During the meal they got to know each other properly for the first time, with Phil confessing that he had had an affair with his sister-in-law Sharon and telling Kathy that she was the one he had always fancied. Wandering along the banks of the Seine afterwards they were jostled by a crowd of people getting off a boat and thrown into one another's arms. It was all very sweet and romantic, just the sort of stuff I love. When they got back to the hotel Phil was obviously imagining that they would be going to the same room, but after a tender goodnight kiss Kathy took out her key and went to her own bedroom door, saying something along the lines of 'Yeah, it's been a lovely evening, but let's take this one step at a time.' I inserted the key in the lock and tried to turn it, but nothing happened. I looked back at Steve and gave him another tender 'Goodnight', while I tried to force the key to turn, with no result except for an unsuitable expletive from Kath. When we got back to England we both received release forms from the BBC asking us to give them permission to use the cock-up on their *Auntie's Bloomers* programme.

To get all the shots they needed of us boarding and disembarking from ferries we had to go across the channel three times. On one of the crossings it was a bit rough. I started to feel very much the worse for wear and was finished off completely when lunch was proudly served up to us – plates full of luscious prawns and other seafood delights. We stayed the first night in Folkestone in a hotel which really was pretty terrible. I felt so uncomfortable in my room that I spent the night in Letitia's, with several other members of the team who were equally reluctant to leave. On the coach down to Paris I was so exhausted I flaked out completely and never knew that Colin, one of the dressers, was taking a picture of me sprawled open-mouthed in my seat, until I woke up and he showed me the Polaroid, threatening to send it in to *The Big Breakfast* where they love producing that sort of thing and asking, 'Is this you?' When we arrived in France we were amazed when a man introduced himself to us and showed us his products, bottles of wine called 'EastEnders'.

Although I lack self-confidence I am very extrovert. I've always enjoyed being on TV game shows, for instance. I went on *Blankety Blank* a few times with Les Dawson, which was a laugh, but the one I enjoyed most was *Give Us a Clue*, which was hosted by Michael Parkinson and had Lionel Blair and

Liza Goddard as team captains. I did three of them and I felt I was really in my element, getting so involved I would completely forget where I was, mugging away like Norman Wisdom while trying to work out what the other team were doing, tripping over my own tongue in my haste to shout out the answers when I knew them, and sometimes when I didn't. Lionel Blair was always taking the mickey with comments like 'Here she comes, the Cockney sparrow!' To me it was just like playing games with the family at a party or on Christmas Day. That sort of thing takes me right out of myself.

While we were waiting for the case against the *Sun* to come to court Kim had a baby and took maternity leave from the police force, which meant that she was going to be able to be around to support me with the others. The family closed in around me. If I ever told Mum on the phone in the morning that I was feeling a bit cheesed off, by the time I got home from work there would be a string of messages on my machine from the others, wanting to know if I was all right.

Not every story in the press was bad. The *Sunday People* asked Geoff and me if we would like to take Jessica to meet Father Christmas in Lapland, taking a reporter and photographer along to record whatever happened. Initially I wasn't keen because I'm not comfortable with that sort of publicity stunt and I wasn't sure that Jess was old enough to enjoy it. But we were all feeling very low about the impending case and I thought it was too good a chance to miss, so we accepted. I'm glad we did.

It was a dream-like trip. I never have really grown up and this was like a fantasy come true, the perfect Christmas experience. They took us over to this place with little log cabins in the woods. Inside we had bunk beds, log fires and saunas, and outside the snow was so heavy the trees were bowing under the weight, just like on Christmas cards. We got around in a snow taxi with Jess and me cuddled in front and Geoff standing behind scooting us along. There was also a ride with some huskies and one evening when Jess was asleep we left her with a babysitter and went out for an hour and a half on a snowmobile, a sort of motorbike on skis which goes through the snow like a speedboat over waves. There were only about two hours of light a day, finishing around two in the afternoon, and during the hours of darkness the woods were lit by globe-shaped street lamps which gave off a sort of beige-coloured light. When the snow flakes were falling in this light it gave the place a strange, eerie, mystical feel. When the time came to visit Santa we all got into a sleigh in our furry hats and boots, with Jessie tucked in between us, covered up by deerhide blankets and pulled by reindeer for about forty-five minutes through the forests. At one point we spotted Santa through the trees and went searching for him. When we finally reached Santa's house his reindeer were waiting outside and there were candles planted in the snow to light our way. Jessie was a bit frightened when she came face to face with Santa, but it was still an amazing experience for all of us, a magical break from the reality which was waiting for us back in London.

16

Fighting Back

It was over a year before the case came to court, and it felt like a very long year. Geoff and I were rowing a lot and there were many moments when it looked as if we wouldn't still be together by the time the case actually came up. The bills kept coming from the solicitors, a few thousand here and a few thousand there, and the months continued to drag by. I became very depressed at times. 'Once this case is all over, darling,' Mum would say, 'you'll be able to start life afresh and you'll feel much better.' The whole family encouraged me to keep going, certain that we would win and be able to get on with our lives again, having cleared the Taylforth name.

To begin with the case was supposed to be heard at the end of 1993, then it was postponed to the beginning of 1994. It was hard to think about or plan anything else with something so frightening hanging over our heads.

When we eventually got our dates to appear in Court Thirteen, Geoff and I went to stay with Mum so that we could be together as a family. We also wanted her to look after Jessie during the days. All my sisters were going to be in the courtroom for the whole trial, but I didn't want Mum to be there more than she had to. The solicitors had warned us that the opposition would be saying some pretty bad things about me to try to blacken my character and I didn't want Mum to have to sit through that unless it was strictly necessary. I knew that she would insist on being there unless I asked her to do me a favour and look after Jess. She was going to have to come to give evidence herself and she was very frightened at the prospect, worried that she would forget something important and let us down. The pressure on her must have been terrible, especially since she didn't have Dad to lean on. Because I was so upset by everything she felt she had to be strong for my sake, but she must have needed a shoulder to cry on as much as I did some nights.

As the case drew closer, I had terrible trouble sleeping and I couldn't eat. I began to lose weight and everyone commented on how bad I looked. Before long I was unable to keep anything down even if I did eat. I was getting the sweats and palpitations and passing out unexpectedly. It was like having the worst sort of stage fright twenty-four hours a day. I went to see a stomach specialist and he told me that it was simply stress. Geoff developed very similar symptoms. Everyone in the family was suffering with us. Kim was falling back on her religion, praying for us and even fasting for a day to prepare herself for the ordeal we were about to undergo. We knew that the media attention was going to be enormous, and I felt very nervous about being scrutinised so closely by the whole world. Usually when I appeared in front of twenty million people it was as Kathy Beale. This time there wouldn't be anyone to hide behind – this was going to be Gillian Taylforth on display. Apart from anything else, what are you supposed to wear on occasions like this? Like all women I have a wardrobe full of stuff but 'never have anything to wear', and I felt that I should probably have something different each day. In the end I dug out all the outfits I had bought recently for weddings and family do's, like a plain black skirt suit with white stitching for the first day.

We arrived at the High Court in the Strand a bit early on the first morning and had to wait with the crowds milling around outside before we were let in. An old man came up to us and introduced himself as 'Courtroom Jack'. Ever since he had retired from his job, he explained, he had spent his time in courtrooms watching cases. 'The judge you've got, Justice Drake, is quite fair,' he told us. 'You'll be all right with him.' The support which we got from everyone there helped a great deal. I felt that we weren't necessarily alone against the world, that perhaps there was more of the world on our side than we had realised.

Eventually we were allowed in and walked past George Carman, the *Sun*'s QC, and the police lawyers to get to our seats. The jury were going to be sitting on one side of the court and the press on the other; our friends and family would sit behind us. On the first day George Carman started trying to introduce any number of new arguments and Michael Beloff got them all thrown out. I was impressed by his performance; he seemed to be right on top of everything and running rings around the *Sun*'s team. Justice Drake seemed to be becoming impatient with the *Sun* and all the nonsense that they wanted to introduce as evidence. They had dug up every newspaper cutting that had ever existed, with all the different stories that other people had made up about me over the years, but they were nearly all thrown out. Despite my nerves I was beginning to feel more optimistic.

On the second day came the reconstruction, in which we all had to demonstrate whether or not it was possible to do what we had been accused of doing in a Range Rover. Geoff's car was parked in the car park at the centre of the court complex and the press photographers were locked out behind the gates in the street. Our solicitors had to put up umbrellas and hold them out to protect us from the long lenses of the cameras which poked through the bars. The facts no longer mattered, the media just needed copy, any copy, and pictures, to keep fuelling their apparently endless appetite for this ridiculous non-story. The reconstruction was like a God-given photo-opportunity from which they were not pleased to be excluded.

Eight men and four women jurors solemnly trooped out into the courtyard with us, plus the judge, six barristers, solicitors and press. The lawyers had taken their wigs off for the occasion. They all circled round the car, trying to get a good view. Geoff and I got in first, both feeling very self-conscious. Geoff sat bolt upright, as he had been on the day, while the jury stared at us through the windows. I was wearing my seat-belt, also as I had been on the day. The judge said that Geoff did not need to undo his trousers for the re-enactment. A few minutes later two employees of the *Sun* climbed into the seats and PC Talbot, the policeman who had made the accusations in the first place, told them what positions to get into to show how he had allegedly found us. The girl buried her head in the man's lap as the onlookers all took turns peering in. Her head was shaking as she suppressed a fit of giggles. The man wasn't able to hide his smirk. The girl did not have her seat-belt done up. When she tried to do the same thing with the belt on she found it was impossible.

As they emerged with red faces, the girl and I had to stand together to check that our heights were similar. 'This is so embarrassing, isn't it?' she said, laughing.

'What,' I replied, 'more embarrassing than working for the *Sun*?' I didn't feel like laughing by then.

'This re-enactment cannot be exact,' Mr Carman piped up, 'because the man's penis was not exposed.' The next day the *Sun* printed the headline 'Yes, you can do it in a Range Rover,' neglecting to point out that you couldn't if your seat-belt was done up.

Now it was my turn in the dock. I was up there for seventy minutes, feeling that the eyes of the whole world were on me alone. It was far more gruelling than being on any stage or in front of any cameras, because I had no idea what was going to be said to me, what questions I would be asked or how I would react. There was no way I could prepare myself for what was about to happen. I did not have the support of scriptwriters or a director who would let me rehearse and reshoot if I got something wrong.

Justice Drake was very kind, seeing that I was shaking with nerves – he could probably hear my knees knocking together – and asked if I wanted a chair. I said I would be all right, but I didn't feel that confident. I could see Geoff watching me, his face set and stern. William Garnett and Michael Beloff stared at me impassively as I talked. I put my side of the story and I hope I never have to go through such an experience again. I couldn't stop myself crying as I told how outraged and distressed I had been when the story appeared, how I had felt unclean and ashamed when I hadn't even done anything. My voice was faltering as I spoke and I wasn't sure that I would be able to keep going. 'An indecent act would have been the last thing on my mind,' I explained. 'Geoff and I were not at that stage in our relationship. I had had a baby four months earlier and I didn't fancy sex for a long time afterwards.' I also admitted that I had been very annoyed with Geoff for his behaviour that day. 'I wasn't in a lovey mood,' I said. 'I wasn't in a passionate mood. We were hardly talking for most of the afternoon.' Mr Carman asked me if I thought I was an accomplished actress. I said I supposed I was. He said that when Kathy was raped by

James Wilmott-Brown I had had to speak lines about how I felt outraged and cheapened and disgusted and humiliated.

'I can't remember the lines now,' I said. 'A rape victim would feel like that though, wouldn't she?'

'I suggest that your performance this morning in the witness box,' he said, 'was very similar to what you had to say when playing the part of a rape victim.'

'No, Mr Carman,' I replied, 'that was Kathy Beale. I am Gillian Taylforth.'

'Did you rehearse what you had to say this morning?'

'No I didn't. I was asked how I felt . . . that was how I felt.' I was furious at the suggestion that because I was an actress, I must be a liar. I could feel tears welling up again and my voice cracking. I felt insulted. 'I'm a human being, flesh and blood,' I protested. 'That is what I am today.'

'I suggest,' he added, 'that Geoff Knights dared you to give him a blow job on the A1. I suggest you had your mouth engaged around his penis and you were moving your head up and down, backwards and forwards, in order to masturbate him. You were giving a blow job on the A1 because you both had a merry day and had some drink. It was a silly indiscretion that went wrong.'

'No,' I said, as calmly as I could, 'that is not the case.'

He also suggested that I had brought the libel action simply for the money I might receive in damages. 'It has never been about the money,' I told him. 'It is to clear my name.' He suggested that I had been expecting an out-of-court settlement from the *Sun* and that Geoff had said he would buy me a house with his damages. He asked me if I agreed that oral sex was a subject freely discussed in women's magazines. I said I supposed it was, although I couldn't remember reading any of the articles.

When Michael Beloff took over he asked me again how

I had felt when the article appeared and I went on to explain all the incidents which had happened to me in the street since then, the sniggers and insults and innuendoes. I told the court about the two young men in suits who had approached me in Borehamwood High Street after I came off the set one day. One of them had unzipped his trousers and shouted, 'Any chance of a quick blow job, Kath?' I explained that I had felt both repulsed and terrified. I told how I had considered leaving the series to get out of the public eye and how my family had persuaded me not to, begging me not to let myself be beaten so easily. When I got back to my seat Geoff kissed me tenderly on the cheek. I felt so relieved that I had finished in the box, it was as if all the tension which had built up inside me over the previous months had been released and I could relax, at least a little, despite what was going on all around. It was someone else's turn to get up there and shake.

The following day the media were full of the story and everyone in the country seemed to agree that we couldn't have done it. But I knew that things were going to change once people heard what the police and Mr Carman had to say. Some of the reporters seemed surprised by the way I spoke. 'Not only does she play Kathy Beale in *EastEnders*,' a woman called Noreen Taylor wrote in the *Daily Mirror*, 'she sounds exactly like her in real life. Instead of the theatrical tones you might expect from an actress there was robust Cockney. In the High Court Gillian let rip just like Kathy would have done had it been her back against the wall; eyes blazing, arms waving, she cried angrily during cross-examination.'

When Geoff was called to the stand they asked him to list his criminal offences. 'All of them?' he asked and a ripple of laughter went round the courtroom. They then dragged up everything he had ever done, right down to when he was fourteen and accused of stealing some drink from a shop and selling it. I couldn't see what relevance it had to something he was being accused of doing when he was thirty-eight, but I suppose they just wanted to blacken his character from the start and make us look like a pair of villains. Mr Carman also made allegations that he had spent nights with 'a former hairdresser' after we had started going together. Geoff admitted that he had visited the woman's home in his Ferrari Testarossa – the press liked that – but had never taken me there. He said he had taken her and two other girls to a nightclub, but had never spent the night with them.

On Friday Barry and Lindsey were called to talk about what had happened at the races, then Mum was called to talk about the state I was in after the incident. I felt so bad for her having to go through it all. I hadn't wanted her to, but she insisted that she wanted to be a witness. Kim was the only one of us who had much experience of courtrooms. I had only been in one once before when I was called to be a witness after a woman ran amok in a pub, attacking other customers, including me. That had been frightening enough, but it was nothing compared to what we were going through now in this packed room. When Janice went up to talk about Geoff going round to her house when he came out of the police station she said out of the blue that she couldn't remember him coming. Our lawyers went into a sudden panic and I couldn't believe what she was saying. Geoff just kept muttering under his breath, 'I was there, I was there.'

It turned out that Janice had been in bed at the time and it was her husband who had let Geoff in, but it was nerve-racking to have doubts cast on our side even for those few moments. Janice realised that she had nearly made things worse for us and I could see that she was close to tears. I felt so awful that she had to be put through this ordeal on my behalf. She told them how the article had affected her life, how one evening she had been in a nightclub when three men approached her. One of them asked, 'Do you give as good a blow job as your sister?' and 'Would you like a trip up the A1?'

Janice, frightened that a fight might break out between these men and the friends she was with, fled from the club, but the men followed her and propositioned her again outside. This time her friends heard them and a fight did break out, ending up with all of them down at the police station.

'I told Gilly several weeks later,' Janice said. 'She broke down and was terribly upset and couldn't stop saying "sorry" to me.'

When we got outside the court Janice and I both dissolved into tears together. William was very calming, telling us not to worry, it was all going to be okay in the end.

Each evening we would go back to Mum's and sit for hours, going over everything that had been said that day, all the things we wished we had thought of at the time, and trying to imagine what would happen the next day. All the family came in to see us and Mum cooked meals that none of us had the appetite to eat. The whole family was angry and stressed and close to breaking point.

Most of the media seemed to be reporting the case well, not distorting our words but putting our case just as we were doing in the court. Ronnie, who wasn't able to get to court because of his job, came up to me at the end of the first week. 'It's going well, isn't it, Gilly?' he said. 'Everyone at work has been reading the papers and they all think you're innocent. The whole country is on your side.'

'I know, Ronnie,' I said, 'but they've only heard our side of the story. Next week the *Sun* and the police are going to be throwing everything they can at us to make us look bad. The media will be reporting things very differently then.' I knew I couldn't afford to get my hopes up too high.

17

The Video

Mum and Dad always brought us up to respect the police, the men in uniform whom you could trust to look after you as long as you were a law-abiding citizen. They were authority figures to us, people who would always give an accurate account of events. Kim had been in the force ten years by then, five of them in the CID, and she had always told us that by and large justice prevailed. In her experience the guilty generally got convicted and the innocent were vindicated. The following week changed our minds completely as we listened to the evidence.

While the policemen talked, explaining in their reasonable tones how it had been, I looked at the jury. I could see that many of them were nodding in agreement, relaxed and secure in their faith in the evidence given by the good old British Bobby. I could understand them thinking that – I might have thought the same if I hadn't been in the car at the time of the incident and known what the true story was. George Carman went on about what wonderful men they were with their commendations for bravery and their years of upstanding service, citing an incident in which PC Talbot faced down a man armed with a Japanese sword. This was supposed to show the jury how much more reliable his word was than ours. Once the caution had been signed at the police station, we were told, Geoff had become very amiable, offering a cigar to one policeman and virtually admitting that we had been having oral sex, saying something like, 'You know how it is, chaps, after a good day out and a few drinks . . .'

When William Garnett told me that George Carman was claiming he had a video which was going to make his case for him, I honestly couldn't think what it could be. I had no recollection of ever making a video that would harm my reputation. If I had done I would have told Michael Beloff when he asked about skeletons in my cupboard. I tried to think back over everything I had ever done in front of a camera so that we could have some warning of what was in store, but I came up with nothing. My conscience was completely clear.

When I discovered what it was I couldn't believe it. Six years earlier a group of Anna Scher's students had gone to the tea bar at the school for a private lunchtime party to celebrate Anna's twentieth year in business, and one of the boys had brought a video camera with him. We had all known each other since we were kids, twenty years in some cases. We were actors and actresses relaxing at a party where we felt confident that it didn't matter what we said or did because we trusted all the other people in the group completely. We were away from the pressures of work, letting our hair down.

There were actors there from many shows, including *Grange Hill*, *The Bill*, *Casualty*, *London's Burning* and *EastEnders*. The party went on all day and the courtroom could follow the passage of time from midday to six in the evening thanks to the clock which hung on the wall at the back of the party. The video started quietly with a speech and the cutting of a birthday cake, but became rowdier as the tape wore on. There were lots of shots of me grinning at the camera and raising my glass. As we watched I tried to remember everything that had happened that day, anything that might show me up in a bad light, but I couldn't think of anything. I was puzzled as to why it was being shown. Before long it was obvious that we were all very drunk and we were messing about. I began to feel a little uncomfortable watching the way I was behaving. It is rather embarrassing to see yourself when you've had a few too many, even if it is six years on, and I wasn't sure that I wanted Mum to have to sit through a demonstration in the cold light of day of the way I and some of my friends might behave at a party. But on balance the video still seemed pretty funny to me. It showed me doing Jimmy Savile impressions, waving a German sausage like a cigar. I also made a few jokes with a bottle when someone else said, 'There's a good head on that bottle' and I replied, 'Yeah, a lot of people say I give good head . . .' In another part of the video I was on the steps outside Anna Scher's. Everyone was geeing everyone else up with jokes and I put the wine bottle between my knees (not 'pressed to my vagina', as Mr Carman repeatedly suggested). Someone then said they hadn't got any money to go to a wine bar. Still doing the Jimmy Savile impression, I joked that I should 'go sell my services on the way – should make £2.50 . . .'

The video lasted for thirty-five minutes. It was embarrassing to watch, but I couldn't believe that anyone was taking it seriously, or that the jury would for a moment think that it had any connection with the case they were trying. I couldn't really understand why it had been allowed as evidence, it seemed so irrelevant.

'This will mean you'll have to go back into the witness box,' William warned me and I felt all the knots in my stomach tighten up; my whole body began to shake with nerves. Once I was back up in front of the court I couldn't stop the tears from coming, but now the judge no longer seemed sympathetic. I could see Geoff sitting on the front bench, gazing down at the floor, boiling with anger, his fists wedged against his teeth as if forcing his fury to stay inside.

With a completely straight face, George Carman proceeded to suggest that this proved I was quite happy to prostitute myself for £2.50. The suggestion seemed so laughable I couldn't believe that anyone would be able to keep a straight face, but the press just copied down his words without a smile and out they came in print the next day. Four of the boys in the video had gone off in a different car to us, with the camera, and started to talk very lewdly about some of the girls – luckily not me – and what they would like to do with them. Some of their suggestions were shocking, but they were nothing to do with me, they were just men's dirty talk. Carman, however, had shown the whole video to the jury, creating the impression that the scene in the car was part of the same thing.

As soon as he saw the video, Justice Drake seemed to change his attitude towards us completely, apparently agreeing with George Carman that this piece of evidence was enough to prove that I was someone who had no reputation to lose, that I was 'no lady when in drink' and was therefore the sort of person who might have behaved in the way that had been alleged. I couldn't understand why this piece of evidence had been allowed when all the newspaper stories had been thrown out. How could a private video, taken six years before, prove that I was the sort of person who would give someone a blow job on the A1? I wanted to say that I was shocked by what the boys were saying in the car, but I thought that would make it sound as if I was trying to pass the blame off on to them. Luckily Michael Beloff made the point that I hadn't been in the car with them while that was going on.

George Carman asked me whether I thought simulating oral sex with a sausage was 'acceptable behaviour'.

'I'm not saying it is,' I replied, 'but I was very drunk at the time and it was just a joke with friends.' I remembered William's advice to look at the jury as much as possible to win their sympathy and trust. I wanted to say to Carman, 'Haven't you ever been to a party, Mr Carman? Have you no idea what happens when people have had a few drinks?' I wanted to say that I was in no way simulating oral sex, that I had merely put the sausage to my mouth like a cigar. I wanted to say that if any member of the jury took anything in the video as anything other than a bit of fun they seriously needed to see a doctor, but William had warned me at the beginning of the trial at no stage to be cheeky to the judge, George Carman or the jury, so I held my peace. Even now I still run through that video in my head when I am lying awake in bed at night, and think of all the things I should have said but didn't think of. I should have been much more assertive, but I was frightened that they would accuse me of being rude to them; I should have been furious that it had been allowed, I should have stood up for myself, but I listened to all the advice I was given and trusted that justice would prevail and the jury would see through Mr Carman's tricks.

'By anyone's standards,' he went on, 'for a young woman in a public place in daylight to put a wine bottle near her vagina after placing it near her bottom and then simulating masturbation is pretty disgusting behaviour.'

'Had I been sober,' I agreed, 'it would not have happened. It was not very nice, no.'

'The whole impression of your evidence – the clothes worn, the tears shown, the language selected, the expressions of outrage and disgust you have shown the jury – I suggest all that has been a great show, misleading the jury, and the true Gillian Taylforth when in drink emerges on that video.'

'I'm sorry,' I was trembling with anger and my voice was cracking, 'you are wrong, Mr Carman.'

I had to agree that I had simulated masturbation with a bottle in the street, but there was no one about. I had not simulated anal sex and I had not gone on to undo my blouse as he suggested. I just went on stressing that we were all very, very drunk and in high spirits. The police lawyer claimed there was a children's playground opposite the steps we were larking about on, but it was six o'clock on a Sunday evening, there was no one about anywhere, and the playground was down a dip and not visible from the road anyway. When I was finally able to go back to Geoff from the stand he cupped my face in his hands and kissed me on the cheeks.

I was so sorry that Mum had to sit through the proceedings that day and witness my ordeal. Although it was obvious to everyone that I was joking and messing about on the video, it was still embarrassing to watch. I was also very disappointed to think that someone should have been able, on whatever terms they had agreed, to make public a video of what was a private party. Mum was very kind about it and said she could see it was just fooling around and innuendo, but the things that George Carman called me when he had me back in the stand made her cry, even when she recalled them months later. George Carman seemed to take everything that anyone else said and give it a whole new, salacious meaning, with choice phrases like 'an open mouth over an erect penis . . . going up and down, up and down'. Kim, who has sat through a lot of trials in her time in the police force, said that it sounded like a defence council talking in a rape case. If this is the sort of ordeal that a girl has to go through to bring a rapist to justice, there is something very wrong with our system. I felt that I was being talked about like a slab of meat. I felt dirty and degraded. I could see the press scribbling down every word that was said and wondered what everyone must think of me. I felt so low as I squeezed Geoff's hand and leaned against him for comfort. He was very supportive when I was near the edge, but at other moments during the trial I could sense the anger boiling up inside him and I tried to calm him down before he exploded over someone and made everything a hundred times worse.

The next day, on the way to court in a taxi, I saw the newspaper headlines on the vendors' billboards and outside the newsagents: 'The actress and the sausage.' I felt so stretched and tired and unhappy I just broke down and cried. 'This is what it's going to be like now for ever, isn't it?' I sobbed. In fact it was far worse than I could have imagined. The papers were just filled with jokes about me and sausages and wine bottles. The *Sun* held a limerick contest, asking readers to make up rude rhymes about me and the 'Taylforth sausage', like playground bullies picking on someone just for the fun of humiliating them in public. Of course it isn't hard to think up an appropriate rhyme for 'Gilly'.

On Thursday George Carman closed the case for the *Sun*: 'It may be, members of the jury,' he announced, 'that the unfortunate words of Gillian Taylforth, uttered no doubt in jest, on a film which she never thought would see the light of day – "I give good head" – may summarise what happened that night. It may be her epitaph.'

He went on to describe how Michael Beloff had presented me attractively in the witness box, sympathetically putting me forward me as a lady suffering from enormous distress over the suggestion that I should stop and have oral sex with a partner after a drunken day out at Ascot.

'Her baby, Jessica, was waved in and out of the script as if Miss Taylforth was president of the Mothers' Union.' I dug my nails into the palms of my hands, feeling the anger boiling up inside me. Even to have Jessica's name brought up in court was almost more than I could bear. How dare he suggest that I had used her just to enhance my image? 'But you know, ladies and gentlemen of the jury,' he continued, 'that was not the true and whole picture of Gillian Taylforth.' He said the video showed that I was capable of sexual coarseness in front of others. He went on to suggest that Geoff and I had stopped for our 'sexual adventure' by the side of the road, 'probably as a dare', thinking that the traffic would go straight past. When we were surprised by PC Terence Talbot, we had to concoct a story about Geoff being ill.

He then suggested that Geoff, 'not a complete stranger to the law', had been the root of the trouble because of his aggressive behaviour to PC Talbot. He also said that Geoff and I might have thought that the *Sun* was an 'easy target'.

The following day Michael Beloff answered with his summing up, warning the jury not to be distracted by George Carman's 'magician's tricks', describing him as a 'past and present master' of the art of distracting juries from the evidence. 'He's the Torvill and Dean of advocacy rolled into one, but with this important difference – straight sixes for style, straight zeros for content.

'Mr Carman's final speech in a libel action is always a source of entertainment – especially if you hear it for the first time. But I would sooner take lessons on family values from Cinderella's ugly sisters.'

Rather than the case being a re-run of the rape scene from *EastEnders*, as Mr Carman had suggested, Michael said he thought it was more like a vintage episode from *Rumpole of the Bailey*. He accused Mr Carman of performing a Perry Mason stunt by suddenly producing a so-called vital piece of evidence at the eleventh hour and the fifty-ninth minute . . . it came in the form of a tacky video shot at a party . . . 'Perry

Mason would produce a firework. Mr Carman has produced a damp squib,' he said. 'When Perry Mason produced his firework, the witness tended to crumble, but Miss Taylforth remained unbowed.'

He insisted that the jury should believe our story that Geoff had opened his trousers in the car to relieve stomach pains. 'Any man who wants sex will open his trousers,' he admitted, 'but not all men who open their trousers want sex.

'Has any credible explanation been advanced by the *Sun* as to why this couple should have had sex beside the A1? It is not exactly Lovers' Lane, is it? With the exception of Wembley Stadium, Hammersmith Palais or Parliament Square, it's about the last place in the country that anyone would select for love-making. A jape, a dare? As John McEnroe used to say, "You cannot be serious."'

The QC representing the police, Richard Rampton, also spoke for the first time that day, accusing me of 'doing a runner' to save my job. He suggested I was worried about what being caught in the act would do to my career and so made up the excuse of having to go back for Jessica. He insisted we had invented the whole story of Geoff's illness as well, asking the jury to consider why PC Talbot should 'concoct such an idiotic story', and suggesting that if Geoff had really been ill I would have insisted on going to the station with him.

By then I was like a victim of shell-shock, hardly taking in what was going on around me, but everyone kept telling me that they thought we were going to win, or at least have a hung jury. Then the judge started to sum up and he seemed to be virtually telling the jury that we were the guilty ones, not to be believed. I found it hard to listen to everything he had to say, he seemed to talk for hours, much of it recapping things that had already been said. I tuned in and out and heard various snatches of what he was saying as he explained the legal situation to the jury.

'So, who must prove the case, how must it be proved and what must be proved in order for you [the jury] to reach your verdict? This is an action in which the two plaintiffs claim an award of money, called "damages", on the grounds that the defendants who publish the *Sun* have falsely damaged their characters and reputations. To attack someone's character is, in legal language, to defame them. You may defame someone either by speaking, by saying something about them, or by writing something. If it is spoken it is called slander; if it is written or broadcast on the radio or television, then it is called libel. This is an action for libel, therefore, since it depends on what was written and published in the *Sun*.

'A defamatory statement is simply one which tends to harm a person's reputation in the eyes of ordinary, reasonable people. The test is, very simply, would the words in the article tend to make ordinary, reasonable people – people like yourselves if you like – think the less of the plaintiffs? That is the test of what is defamatory.

'In some cases there is a dispute about what the words really mean and whether or not they would make people think less of the plaintiffs. In those cases it is for the jury to decide what the words mean and whether or not they are defamatory. There is often a lot of argument about that. In this case, there is not; the *Sun* did publish these words. It is perfectly clear what they mean: that the plaintiffs were committing a sexual act in a public place, and no one disputes that they are defamatory. So you do not have to bother with those questions.

'But, a plaintiff cannot recover damages for something which is defamatory if it is true. If you call a man a thief that is to make people think the less of him, but he cannot recover damages if he is one. It is a complete answer to publishing a defamatory article to show that it is true, and that is to say, to show that it is true in the essential matters . . . The main thing is that in order to provide a defence to an action for defamation, the defendants have to prove that the real essence – the guts – of the attack on the plaintiffs is true; in this case that there was a sexual act committed in that Range Rover.'

So we were to be judged on that. It came down to whether they believed an actress liable to be a bit coarse after a few drinks and her boyfriend who had a criminal record, or the police.

'What you have to decide in this case is,' the judge was still talking on, 'do you think it more likely than not that the defendants have proved that the sex act did take place? Have they proved on balance of what is likely that the article is in its essentials true?'

He talked and he talked and he talked. 'Obviously, at the end of the day, your final verdict depends on whether you prefer the evidence of PC Talbot as to what he says he saw, or the two plaintiffs who say that he must be lying because he could not have seen what he says he saw because they were not doing it.' My attention drifted away for a while and then returned as he said, 'The video of Miss Taylforth at the party in 1988 has nothing at all to do with what happened on Ascot Day 1992, but it is possible it may assist you by helping you to judge the truthfulness and the reliability of Miss Taylforth's evidence. It is what lawyers call evidence as to credit or credibility. Its only use in this case is (as the defendants would say) to help you to judge Miss Taylforth's truthfulness. It does not affect her reputation.' The headlines in the papers, I thought, suggested that perhaps the public showing of the video had had some effect on my reputation.

Eventually he stopped and adjourned the court until the Monday, when he intended to take up where he had left off. We were left hanging in limbo, exhausted but unable to sleep, weakened but unable to eat, not knowing whether we were going to win or lose, sick with worry and fear, regretting that we had ever started on the case. On Sunday Peter Hillmore wrote a piece in the *Observer* in which he questioned Mr Carman's accusation that I was two different people: the demure person who sat in court every day and a totally different person outside. The same, he suggested, could be said of Mr Carman himself.

'It is difficult to imagine the demure QC being the same person when he is not standing up in court wearing a wig made from the tail of a horse. Barristers do not, for example, tell their wives they "will brook no delay" or warn their children against "animadverting". And when Mr Carman feels queasy, it is almost impossible to imagine that he will talk about "discharging his vomit" or "evacuating" – terms that he used last week.'

He ended the article: 'At times, the jury has been in on a *Horizon* medical special, listening to detailed debate as to exactly where Mr Knights "discharged his vomit" after feeling ill, as he claims. And exactly what kind of vomit it was. Or indeed whether he vomited at all, as PC Talbot said Mr Knights did not. Next episode tomorrow.'

He was right. Our nightmare seemed like one huge soap opera to everyone out there following it in the papers and on the television.

We returned to court on Monday morning, fighting through the crowds to get inside, dazed with tiredness from sleepless nights and worry. The judge continued to sum up, repeating everything that PC Talbot had told us in the court.

'"The light was perfect, with still some sun. I got out. I put my hat on and walked up the offside of the Range Rover in the road. I could at first see only one person, a man in the passenger seat, just the top of his head and shoulders. I could not see a driver at all. I walked up the offside of the vehicle and looked through the driver's window and saw a woman with blonde hair lying across with her head in the man's lap and her head was moving up and down. The man had his eyes closed. I tapped on the window. He turned and I saw for a fleeting moment he was holding his erect penis in his right hand and then he was trying to put his penis into his trousers. I have no doubt," he said when asked, "that I saw an erect penis. I had no motive to make that up."' And so the whole story which I so vehemently denied was repeated yet again for the world to hear.

18

The Verdict

The jury were supposed to come out and decide on the Monday, but they didn't, they just had one more question. They wanted to know whether, if Geoff had signed the caution form at the police station simply to get out, knowing as he signed that it accused us of outraging public decency, we would still have been able to bring a libel case. If he had admitted it, whether or not we had actually done it, would we have been able to bring our claim?

'If the jury finds for the plaintiffs on that basis,' Carman said, 'I will demand a re-trial.'

I thought, I couldn't go through this again, as the jury went back out to deliberate on this reply. Geoff and I were wandering around in the High Court for ages, waiting for the result. I just wanted to find out the verdict and go home. While we were waiting a man came up and introduced himself. 'I've been here from day one,' he said. 'I wanted to follow the trial because I was stitched up by the police and I never got any justice. I wanted to see justice done for you, even though I couldn't get it myself.' I thanked him, but didn't feel encouraged. I never wanted to step inside that building again as long as I lived. Dinah, William's assistant, said she would let us know when the jury were back. Eventually she poked her head over the balcony and shouted down to us.

'The jury's gone home. The judge has let them go because they can't make up their minds.'

My knees gave out under me and I collapsed into Geoff's arms, sobbing. I had geared myself up to going back home that night and, win or lose, never having to return to that court again, but now we would be back in there in the morning, after yet another sleepless night. Geoff supported me to a chair and brought me some water.

'The longer they take,' William had told us, 'the better your chances. If they had come straight back in you would have lost.'

On the Tuesday morning when we arrived there were the usual crowds outside, cheering us on: 'Good luck, Kath'; 'We're with you, Kath!' they called out as we passed. I recognised a lot of their faces.

The jury finally came back in and asked the same question as they had the day before. This time Justice Drake stepped in. 'Perhaps,' he said, 'I can be of help. If you are asking if Mr Knights did sign that caution, knowing that he was being cautioned for outraging public decency, and he has been lying to the court, then we will call it perjury and Miss Taylforth and Mr Knights will have perjured themselves in court.' I looked askance at William, who shrugged, as if to say he didn't know what the judge was talking about. 'So, members of the jury, if you do find for the plaintiffs on this basis I will want to know why and I will have to decide whether to have a re-trial or bring Mr Knights to court for perjury.'

Later that day the jury returned again and the judge asked if they were unanimous – they weren't, but there were now only two people who disagreed with the majority.

The jury were finally there, ready to give their verdict as I sat in the court with Dad's fob watch in my hand. I had kept it with me all through the trial as a lucky mascot, as well as wearing Mum's bracelet and Nan's ring. Geoff had insisted on wearing an old shirt that his nan had given him, that he was convinced was lucky for him. Because we hadn't been expecting to go back to court again that day he had had to ask Mum to wash it out for him overnight. It was an old mauve nylon thing with a hole in the elbow, but he wouldn't go into court without it.

'Have you reached a decision?'

'Yes, we have . . .'

William had said to me earlier that if I felt I was getting too upset and couldn't cope I should leave the court, because the press were watching me like vultures, eager to pounce. As I waited for the verdict I looked round the room: it was packed, with reporters lining up along the walls, all waiting to see what the outcome would be so that they could rush to phone through their headlines. I could see my family all waiting as well.

'We find for the defendants.'

A gasp went round the crowd. 'What?' No one seemed able to believe what they had just heard. We had lost.

'What bloody lodge do you belong to?' Kim shouted at the judge.

I could feel my heart beating faster and I began to panic, sure that I was about to have an asthma attack. I couldn't get my breath. George Carman was standing up, cool and businesslike, asking the judge about costs.

William saw what was happening to me. 'Get outside,' he said. As I stood up I turned round and saw Geoff's mum and dad looking round in disgust at everyone and I saw all my sisters, angry and shouting. 'Get her out now.' William's voice sounded more urgent this time. Geoff started to help me to the door, but my legs went from under me. I could feel that he was dragging me along, but it all seemed distant, as if it was happening to someone else.

Kim jumped to her feet. 'This is what British justice has done to my sister!'

Debbie ran up to Sergeant Cole, one of the policemen who had given evidence, and shouted, 'Are you satisfied now, are you?' He just smirked and walked off and the press printed that she had shouted it at the jury.

As Geoff, Sara and my sisters swept me out of the court, the press closed in with their cameras flashing. They managed to get me up some stairs, through one set of double doors into a corridor and then we came to another set with a security guard on them. As Geoff laid me down to rest I could see reporters forcing their way through the doors to get to us. Janice pushed the doors back to keep them away. She didn't realise that they swung both ways and they went straight into a photographer's face. The levels of shouting and pushing seemed to build up all around me. All I kept saying to Geoff was 'I can't believe ten people think we did it. I can't believe it.' I turned to William. 'They're saying I'm guilty.'

'No,' he corrected me, 'they are not saying you are guilty of any criminal act. You brought a civil case against the *Sun*, accusing them of ruining your reputation. The jury is saying that you have not proved that the *Sun* was guilty of ruining your reputation when they printed this story.'

I tried to stand up and get away, but my legs wouldn't work and I was having more and more trouble breathing. I just didn't seem to be able to fill my lungs. Geoff held me and tried to calm me. Everyone was gathering round and Janice was shouting at Geoff, suggesting ways to get me breathing. As I passed out I heard Janice let out a horrifying scream, 'Nooooo!' Later they told me it was because she thought I was dead. Apparently my lips and fingertips had gone blue.

They rolled me over and someone punched me in the chest to start me breathing again.

The next thing I knew I was on the floor with paramedics leaning over me. They lifted me on to a chair and carried me to an ambulance. I kept saying, 'Don't tell Mum, don't tell Mum . . .'

'You'd better tell her,' Sara said, 'because it's going to be on the news and she'll hear it that way.' Kimmie came in the ambulance with Geoff and me. The reporters were all holding their cameras up to the windows, trying to get shots of anything they could.

'Look at them,' one of the paramedics said. 'They're disgusting.' She held a blanket up to one side of the vehicle to protect me while Kimmie took off the cape she had been wearing and held it up to the other side. Geoff's mum and dad followed in the car while Debbie and Janice drove quickly to find Mum, who was spending the day with my aunt Lil. Mum was in the kitchen when the news came on the television, but Aunt Lil saw it and by the time she broke it to Mum Debbie and Janice had arrived. Mum ran straight out for a taxi and came to the hospital.

When the ambulance arrived at the hospital the press were already there, waiting for us. Kimmie stood in front of me as they lifted me out of the ambulance and the paramedics covered my head with a blanket. 'Perhaps they'll think I'm dead,' I said, 'then they'll leave me alone.' One of the photographers pushed Kimmie out of the way, which was a bad move since she taught self-defence for the police and she punched him.

The man staggered back, shouting angrily, 'I'm calling the police!'

Kimmie pulled out her badge and flashed it at him. 'I am the f. . .ing police!' I was taken into a room and a few minutes later Kimmie came in crying. 'Look, Gilly.' She gave me a bunch of flowers. 'This is how much you're loved.'

'Where'd you get them from?' I asked.

'There's a fan, he's followed us from the court – John Cohen – he's an old chap and he's brought you these. He said not to give up because there's a lot of people out there who support and love you.' I thought that was so lovely. Another fan, Nick Curtis, told me later that when he saw the verdict in a newspaper he broke down and cried in the shop and had to be consoled by the newsagent. Nick has been a wonderfully loyal and supportive fan ever since the days of *The Rag Trade*, regularly bringing cards and presents for me and Jessica round to Mum's place.

The reporters still didn't give up and kept getting into the hospital under different pretexts, so Geoff stood guard on the door and ushered them out again. They were all trying to bait him and make him lash out and live up to the reputation they had given him as a hard man. The *Evening Standard* dedicated its entire first three pages to the story: 'EastEnder star loses – actress rushed to hospital after sex in car libel . . . All ended in tears, agony and possible financial ruin . . . in contrast Mr Carman left the scene of his High Court triumph and strolled to a Fleet Street tavern accompanied by his legal team.'

While the headlines might have been screaming out the most lurid things they could think of, some of the editorials inside the papers were more thoughtful and supportive. John Mortimer, author of the *Rumpole of the Bailey* series which Michael Beloff had referred to in his summing up, wrote in the *Evening Standard*: 'The main purpose of our complex, élitist, unjust and unreasonable libel laws is clearly to enrich lawyers and keep the public entertained. Libel actions must fulfil much the same function as the circus in the days of ancient Rome. The miseries of the masses are alleviated by the public suffering of a few and there are a good many laughs to be got along the way.

'Whether lawyers should be ashamed of their fees is another matter. While we allow libel cases to be great theatrical events lawyers will claim star billing and star salaries.'

A few days later in the *Daily Mail*, Jani Allan, who had suffered her own ordeal in a libel action with George Carman as the opposing barrister, said, 'For all his celebration in legal circles is he [George Carman] admired? Professor George Steiner once noted, "If I were ever accused of machine-gunning 12 Salvation Army officers on the streets of London then I would go to George, because I know that he would be the only man able to get me off." Intended, no doubt, as a generous compliment, this comment really says it all.' She went on to compare her experience with mine: 'We are both women and any woman facing George Carman in court does so at her peril. She must prepare herself for the bloodless abattoir and thence almost inevitably the boneyard of damaged reputations.'

19

Into the 'Boneyard of Damaged Reputations'

For months after the case, when I went out in the street or into shops with Jessica, or with Mum, young boys would come up and shout, 'Give us a blow job then, Kath,' and there was nothing I could do about it, because the courts said I deserved it.

Once when Geoff and I drew up at some traffic lights another car drew up alongside and some blokes started shouting 'Gobbler' through the window at me. Everywhere I went I could see people pointing, nodding and whispering to one another. I used to get panic attacks, my blood rushing to my face and my heart pounding. If I was walking down a street and I saw a crowd of boys I had to cross over the road and walk the long way to avoid them and their jeers.

While the case was going on and Jessie was with my mum a reporter approached a fifteen-year-old girl in one of the other flats, offering her £500 and a camera if she would take a picture of Jessie going out with her nan. That's a lot of money to a fifteen-year-old, but luckily she's a lovely girl and she told them she wouldn't do it. But I knew that if we went back to Mum's when I was discharged from hospital the chances were that we would be pestered by the doorbell and phone calls. We needed a sanctuary to go to while things calmed down, and Geoff's parents suggested we go out to them in the country. The press still found out where we were and followed us, but it was harder for them to get close. The house stands with one other in the middle of open fields, making it difficult for anyone to hide close by. The road leading to the house is narrow with no room to park a car. Some of them tried to get photographs by sneaking through the next door neighbour's garden, but the men spotted them and chased them off. Most of them repaired to the car park of a pub about a mile away, from where they could watch the house over the fields with their binoculars and telephoto lenses. We remained inside. I wasn't able to get any clean clothes and had to stay in the same ones for four days, rinsing out my underclothes each night and hanging them on the radiator to dry.

A friend of mine, Jane Moore, who had done the series of articles in *Today* about my having Jessie and who now worked for the *Daily Mirror*, asked if I wanted to sell the *Mirror* my story. We still owed William Garnett's firm some fees and couldn't see how we would be able to pay, so William suggested that he negotiate a sale with the paper and the proceeds could go towards his bill. We thought we might as well, since they were all going to be writing about us anyway.

Jane came out to Pete and Jean's house and was shocked by the way I looked. 'More than a stone has dropped from Gillian's already thin frame,' she wrote, 'and she makes a shocking sight. Her face is shadowed by a lack of sleep. She wrings her hands constantly and falters in a bid to fight back tears.'

Next morning the television was on downstairs, tuned to *This Morning* with Richard and Judy. The subject under discussion was whether or not Geoff and I had been right to bring the case; they were asking people to phone in with their views. Jane was there with us. Mum was watching the show. Some of the callers were saying lovely things, but then someone came on the line and criticised me. Mum began shouting at her, saying things like, 'How dare you talk about my daughter like that? None of you know her!' Then she started shouting about the media and how they were all leeches, even turning on poor Jane. She seemed to be becoming short of breath, as I had done outside the courtroom, then she passed out on the floor. As she lay there, semi-conscious, with all of us crowded round, she kept calling out, 'Ron, where's Ron?' I felt terrible. All she wanted was to have Dad with her to give her a cuddle and tell her everything was going to be all right, but there was nothing we could do to make it happen for her.

When we did finally leave the house to go to a hotel where we could talk to Jane in peace, Geoff and I went in different cars, lying down on the floor with blankets over us. Geoff's dad and brother and a friend blocked the lane at one end, following us and then blocking it again behind us, while Kim and her husband drove the Range Rover off in another direction to lay a false trail. We drove four times round a roundabout to check that we weren't being followed and then sped away. The Range Rover did fool some of them who gave chase for a while. When they realised their mistake and peeled off, Kim couldn't resist pulling the car over to see if she could do what we had been accused of doing with her seat-belt on. She came to the conclusion that it most definitely was not possible.

I was getting to know who my friends were, the ones who wrote to me or rang to ask if there was anything they could do and the few, like Steve McFadden, who turned up at court to support me. Brian May (Anita Dobson's partner and the guitarist from Queen) had been keen to come, but Anita had been worried that there was a danger of turning the whole thing into a media circus, which I quite understood. Some people kept in touch by ringing Mum or other relatives, not wanting to bother me when I had so much on my mind.

I was due back at work, having had two weeks off for the trial, but the producers kindly let me have some more time to recover and I went back the following week. When I walked into my room there were helium balloons everywhere, red hearts with string on the end carrying messages of love and support, all organised by Peter Halston, the costume designer. There were piles of flowers, cards and chocolates and I just cried my eyes out again. I went running down to wardrobe and make-up where they all were to thank them. When I walked out on to the studio floor all the crew shouted their greetings, they were really great.

The articles continue to appear whenever someone feels like writing something, or selling a story to the papers. One man whom I had met a few times in a group of people was quoted at length in a long piece in the *News of the World* about what great sex we had had together. He described in detail how I gave him a blow job. The story went on for pages. In fact I had first met him at one of Michelle Collins's (Cindy in the series) birthday parties. He was a friend of Michelle's and asked to have his picture taken with me – a picture which was then reproduced in the paper to prove how close we were. Later that night a whole group of us had gone back to his place to play Trivial Pursuit until five in the morning. In the same feature two girls came forward and talked about Geoff asking them to give him blow jobs in his various flash cars. I tried to ring the man who was claiming to have been with me to find out why he had done it, but there was no reply. I can guess why, anyway: someone made him an offer he couldn't refuse and he was tempted by the possibility of seeing his name in the papers for a few hours.

I still miss Dad all the time, but I am relieved that he

didn't have to read or hear all this about his daughter. I somehow feel that if he had been alive none of it would have happened, that he would have protected me in some way. Sometimes, of course, the jokes that were published were quite witty, but that didn't make them any less hurtful. Mac, the cartoonist, drew a scene in the BMW boardroom, just after the company took over Rover, who make Range Rovers. 'Gentlemen,' one of the directors is saying, 've haf made a terrible mistake. Apparently our purchase does not include the little blonde Fraulein from *EastEnders*.'

I was in a shop with Geoff and Jessica one Saturday. Jessica was getting bored, so Geoff took her outside. When I turned round and saw he wasn't there I started to shake. I suddenly felt alone, exposed and vulnerable. I just stood there staring at the floor, feeling that everyone was looking at me and pointing. I know they probably weren't, but I just felt the whole world was laughing at me.

Just after the trial we were all at a first birthday party for Ronnie's baby, Chloe, when a phone call came from one of Ronnie's mates telling him that there was a butcher near Smithfield Market who was advertising 'The Taylforth Sausage'. Mum was so upset to think that anyone was using Dad's name like that. Kim rang the police to find out if there was anything we could do and they said we would have to take the butcher to court – well, there was no way any of us wanted anything more to do with the courts. Ronnie was all for going down there with a group of friends and a baseball bat and sorting the butcher out, but we dissuaded him. Geoff had a mate who worked in Smithfield and he assured him that all the blokes in there were furious and that they would sort it out for us. We didn't hear any more about it.

While Kim was on maternity leave from the police she was called by a neighbour of Mum's to help a three-year-old child whose mother had locked him out in the rain with no shoes. When Kim knocked on the door the woman rushed out at her, kicked her and caused her to fall awkwardly on her ankle. The result was that Kim had to be invalided out of the force. The stress of the court case, however, had also caused her to go to see a police psychiatrist, who told her that had she not been medically pensioned off for the injury he would have recommended that she should be for the stress. Kim's faith in the police had been destroyed, just as mine had. She has always been someone who becomes upset on behalf of other people, even strangers whose stories she might read about in the papers, and she took the court ordeal very badly. Her doctor put her on anti-depressant tablets to get through it and she started to visit the police psychiatrist. She told him that she felt betrayed by the police force, which she had always believed to be basically honest.

There's nothing for it now but to get on with my life. One of the managers at the BBC sent me a very nice letter telling me to remember that I was the same Gillian who had walked into the courtroom on the first day, and not to lose sight of that fact. One of the great parts of the job is the letters we all get, sometimes fifteen letters a week, sometimes hundreds. The boys in the series get the most, but we all get cards and presents at Christmas, Easter, Valentine's Day and on our birthdays (Jessica's as well), which is lovely. Some of the letters are addressed to 'Kathy at the café' and the post office still delivers them.

After the trial the letters arrived by the sackful, most of them from kind individuals who wanted me to know that they supported me and thought I had been badly treated. There was one from a hotelier on the Isle of Bute who said that the whole island was shocked by what had happened to me and they all supported me. An army sergeant wrote from a barracks in Scotland saying that they had taken the *Sun* off their 'pro-forma list' as their men did not read 'comics'. They had written 800 letters to the paper expressing their disgust at what had happened. 'It is not the mandate of *any* newspaper to destroy our "dream girls",' he said. I am trying to reply personally to as many of these kind letters as I can, but they arrive by the ton and I can only do a few a day. I hope the people who are having to wait for their replies will understand. I would hate to think that they believed I was not pleased to hear from them. To a large extent it was the letters from strangers assuring me that there were lots of people out there who thought we had been treated badly that helped to keep me going. If I hadn't received so many I might have thought that most people agreed with Mr Carman and Justice Drake.

Of course not all the letters we receive are nice. When the story about Debbie and me being mugged got into a newspaper, about three months after it actually happened, I received a lot of supportive letters and flowers, but also a letter from someone saying they were really glad it had happened and that they were disappointed I hadn't been raped as well and caught some horrible disease: 'We know who you are and we see you shopping up Chapel Market. They may not have got you this time, but we will next time.' Mum was helping me with my fan mail at the time and unfortunately she opened that one. I went to the producers and asked if they would open my post for me and remove letters like that before they got to us.

Right from the start I tried to answer every one personally, which is very time-consuming, though the BBC do pay the postage. When the court case was on and the publicity was everywhere it became impossible to get to them all with hand-written notes, so I asked Carolyn Weinstein –

the producer's secretary and a good friend – to print me up a letter which I could personalise. Nearly thirty people actually sent me money to help me pay off the costs of the court case, which was so touching; one was the author Jilly Cooper, whom I had met on the set once and got on with very well. She said that having met me she knew I hadn't done it, and I guess she knows a lot about media harassment herself. I actually met her first when I was at school and she was still a journalist. She came to hand out the prizes and we had a chat, but I don't think she remembered that when we met again. One person sent a pound sellotaped to a letter and said that if each of my fans did the same I would end up with £17 million, which was a kind thought. Jill Gascoigne rang my agent and suggested that they set up an appeal fund to help me; she was outraged on my behalf. It didn't come to anything, but I was very touched by her concern. Zoe Wanamaker and John Nettles also rang in, and Siân Phillips sent a lovely note. Joe Ashton, the MP, wrote to say he was raising the question of how the information about us got to the press from the police. Chris Biggins wrote saying how appalled he was by what had happened.

When you are in a long-running soap some people do become confused about what is real and what is happening to your character. I often get people in the street calling me Kathy and saying things like, 'Have a word with your son, will you, he's being really horrible to those people.' When I was going out with Nick a lot of people used to wag their fingers at me and say, 'I'm telling your husband on you.' It is sometimes hard to tell how much they are joking and how genuinely confused they are. Kathy's had a few proposals of marriage from fans as well, which is very flattering, and some requests from the army for pin-up pictures – I'm afraid they have to have the usual publicity photographs, which is probably just as well given the shape of me. One fan wrote saying how much they liked the character of Kathy and they thought she should have more storylines, then suggested it might be nice if she was to fall under a bus! Schoolchildren sometimes decide to do projects about us and write asking for information.

When Arthur Fowler lost his job a man came up to Bill Treacher, the actor who plays him, in the street and gave him a card for a security firm, telling him to go and see them because they would treat him well. The day after the public were told that Den was the father of Michelle's baby, when the story was all over the front pages of the tabloids, Bill was walking up the High Street in Borehamwood when a bloke stopped him.

'What do you think, then, Arthur?'

'What?' Bill asked.

'What are you going to do then, with him?'

'Who?'

'Den. He's the father of your Michelle's baby! What are you going to do about it?'

'Well, I don't know about it, do I? They're keeping it from me . . .' Bill protested.

'It's in all the papers!' the man exclaimed, amazed at Bill's innocence.

When Wicksy was having an affair with Ian's wife Cindy, Adam Woodyatt was in his car at some traffic lights one day when a man tapped on the window. Adam wound it down. 'Your best mate's knocking off your wife,' the man told him and walked off.

I must admit that I sometimes have trouble with the dividing line between fantasy and reality myself. When Michelle was supposed to be marrying Lofty we were filming the wedding in a church. She was actually going to jilt him at the altar, but in case the press found out in advance they filmed two versions, one in which she walked out and the other in which she said yes and they walked out together. When they were filming the happy version I just stood there and wept, no acting required. I seem to be unable to stop myself crying at anyone's wedding, even an imaginary one.

Sometimes, when the writers give our characters something to do or say which we don't think is right, we protest. Now that we know our characters so well we are listened to more often than in the past, but in the early days we had to say the lines exactly as they were written. We often reminisce about the worst lines we have had to say. It might make a good party game for people to try to say some of them out loud and sound like a believable person.

Wicksy won the football scratch cards in the pub one week and Nick had to say, 'I've won. I've won. I've won, I've won, I've won.' Once, when some stolen goods were found in a warehouse, Paul Medford, who played Kelvin, had to say, 'This must be some villain's hoard.' Listening to Pauline talking about how Den Watts should be strung up for what he had done to Michelle, I had to respond, 'No jury would convict!' One day just before she disappeared Angie asked me always to look after Sharon for her. A few episodes later Sharon came to me and said, 'I know you always knew Angie as my mum, but did you know my real mum, you know, she who gave birth to me?' Just try saying some of those in Cockney accents.

We all spend a lot of time together at the *EastEnders* firm, much more than in most jobs, and sometimes we grow very close. I always feel most secure when I am with the others, even if we are out in a public place like a nightclub or a restaurant. Being stared at isn't so embarrassing if you are amongst a bunch of people who are all being stared at, and the boys usually get more attention than the girls do in public anyway. We've all been through similar experiences, which leads to a powerful camaraderie. When I heard that Barbara Windsor was going to come in to play my possible future mother-in-law I was really pleased. I had met her a couple of times before because she's a friend of Chris Biggins, and we've always got on well. She knows just what it feels like to have the press hounding you and making up stories, and she seems to be able to rise above it beautifully. On top of everything else she is a really good laugh.

In the months after my trial Steve McFadden started coming to the attention of the media when several girls went to the press with stories about him, which he found very distressing. One weekend, soon after all this press coverage, he was supposed to be going to Cornwall for the weekend, as he often does to relax on the river. But the trip fell through, so he went out for a drink with some of his mates in London. They were down round Waterloo and Steve suggested they should go for a walk along the side of the Thames. They were feeling philosophical, singing a chorus or two of 'Que Sera, Sera', when a group of down-and-outs rushed out at them from one of the 'cardboard cities' under Waterloo Bridge. In the scuffle Steve fell down some steps, hurting his arm, and as he struggled to his feet a man came at him with a knife, stabbing him in several places. He tried to run. Not knowing the area, he headed for the opening which had the most light and luckily it took him away from the scene. If he had picked a dead end by mistake God knows what would have happened to him. I heard about it and rang the hospital. They told me he was okay, but I couldn't speak to him.

'Just tell him Gillian phoned,' I said, 'and that I know some people will do anything to get out of doing scenes with me, but this is going too far.'

Geoff and I try to continue our lives as if nothing unusual has happened, as if we are just a normal couple with a young baby, but the pressure doesn't let up. Geoff was looking for a business opportunity that would help him get back on his feet and an old schoolfriend of his told him about a company he was forming to sell up-market British desserts in Spain. Geoff went down a few times and it looked as if the project had possibilities, so at the end of September he went down for three weeks to set everything up. I had a lot of work to do because we were filming the big scenes when everything in the storyline was coming to a head – Sharon hearing about Phil and Kathy's engagement; Grant finding out about Sharon's affair with Phil – and so there was no opportunity to take any time off. There was a lot for me to learn and it was really quite gruelling shooting some of the scenes. I was also feeling very low with a cold bug which had affected my nose and throat again, but I managed to keep working. After Geoff had been gone a couple of weeks the reporters from the Sunday papers began ringing up. They said they had heard that Geoff had left me and done a runner to Spain, would I like to comment? I told them that it wasn't true, but I no longer cared what they printed. They claimed they had talked to Geoff in Spain and he had said it was over between us.

On the Saturday of that week I was feeling really low, knowing that something would be appearing the next day, but I had to go in to work. I was in the canteen at lunchtime with my sister Debbie when a young woman came up to me. I didn't recognise her at first because she had a blonde wig on.

'You don't know me,' she said, 'my name is Cleo Rocas.' The name rang a bell and I remembered seeing her on *The Kenny Everett Show* some years before.

'Oh, yeah,' I said, 'I remember you, nice to meet you.'

'I just wanted to tell you that I think that you've acted with so much dignity and strength of character about everything. I know so many people who are so full of admiration for you. Those papers don't realise what they've done for you. They've created so much support for you out there.'

I felt the tears welling up. It was just the sort of boost I needed to get me through the rest of the day. I don't think Cleo had any idea what she did for me that afternoon. I went straight home that evening to tell Mum and burst into tears.

'See,' Mum said triumphantly, 'I keep telling you what people think about you.'

On 2 October the *People*'s front page was smothered in the headline 'Gillian's lover runs off to Spain – EastEnders star in tears as Geoff Knights leaves her alone to face more shame'. Inside, the headline was 'From blow job to no job. Now Knights is on the passion cake run in Spain'.

The story was that I had been 'blown out' by Geoff who had gone off to Spain to become 'a cake salesman'. They made the replies which I had given them in anger sound like pathetic whinges and they pointed out that I had been 'receiving psychiatric help' since losing the court case – this referred to the counselling I had been having to try to overcome the anxiety attacks and come to terms with what had happened. They quoted my brother Ronnie as slagging Geoff off for leaving me in the lurch, which he denied having said. They tracked Geoff down to a bar outside Marbella where he denied that the relationship was over. I felt so vulnerable and depressed. I rang Geoff and told him what they were saying. He flew back to be with me on the Tuesday. The moment he arrived in the country the press appeared at the front door, their cars parked up the little cul-de-sac where we now live in a rented house, their cameras firing off every time we went near the door or window. When I walked out to the car it was as if I'd won an Oscar with the lights flashing all around us. They set up a permanent camp, so we had to retreat behind drawn curtains. Mum was coming round one evening and we planned to go out for a meal, but we couldn't face it, so we ordered a pizza in. At one stage Mum went out to plead with the reporters to leave me alone, but they wound her up to such an extent that she ended up shouting at them. I really couldn't understand what was going on – they had done the story and now Geoff was back, there didn't seem to be anything else they could find out.

On the Wednesday they told me that a girl had come forward alleging she had had an affair with Geoff in Spain. 'Would you like to say something?' I had no comment, but they kept ringing the bell, pushing letters through the door and leaving messages on the answering machine. By Saturday I was so desperate we called the police to see if they could clear the press away from the house, but when they arrived they told us there was nothing they could do.

'What would happen,' Geoff said, 'if I hit one of them?'

'We'd have you for assault,' the man replied.

As the police left I saw them stopping for a little chat and a laugh with the assembled press outside and I felt completely trapped and abandoned. The following Sunday we filled the front page of the *People* again: 'My sex fling with Gillian's violent lover – Liar Knights jets back after days of passion'. Inside there was a huge picture of a girl Geoff had supposedly had an affair with and then beaten up: 'We made such wonderful love . . . two days later he smashed me in the face.' Geoff was described as 'fast fisted', with a picture taken by one of the photographers outside the house of him lunging angrily at one of the reporters who kept ringing the doorbell. I could remember the moment well. The doorbell had gone for the hundredth time and Jessica had started crying, saying that the people outside were frightening her. That was the last straw for Geoff and he went for the man, which was exactly what they hoped he would do.

The girl in Spain was quoted as talking about the night Jessica was conceived and other fictitious personal details. To see Jessie's picture in the article and to read the girl's stories about her left me feeling gutted. I couldn't stop crying.

My stomach was playing up one evening while all this was going on and I went downstairs to get myself some Andrews. I remember opening the tin and the next thing I knew I was lying on the floor staring up at the ceiling. A couple of days later the same thing happened at work and I passed out on the set. I seemed to be tired all the time, sometimes going to bed at the same time as Jessica, being asleep by half past eight in the evening. The family were all going on at me for not eating enough but I didn't seem to be able to find my appetite.

On the Monday the *Daily Star* came out with a story from Geoff's old schoolfriend and business partner, claiming that Geoff's antics had ruined his life. By this time I felt so tired and sickened and dazed by the whole thing, so desperate to do the best thing for Jessica, to try to keep the peace with Geoff, to learn all the lines I had to learn for the programme and so drained by my cold I was ready to give up.

20

Battered But Not Broken

It started as a nice night out. The George Hotel, next to Broadcasting House in Portland Place, has a restaurant at the top with dramatic views out across the rooftops of London. Both Geoff and I have been there on several occasions in the past and have got on well with the people who run it, so we were pleased to be invited to a reopening after the restaurant had been revamped and renamed the Heights.

The financial pressures of finding the money to pay the lawyers, coupled with the media attention, have taken a terrible toll on my relationship with Geoff, leading to a lot of arguments. When we are in the privacy of our own home I am more than ready to answer him back, and sometimes I do a bit of nagging myself, but I don't like public scenes. Despite what many people think I am not keen to see myself emblazoned across the front pages of the tabloids for having rows with my boyfriend every night of the week, particularly as the rows are usually about the most ridiculous things.

On this evening, however, we had organised a babysitter for Jess and we were having a really nice time to begin with, just the two of us. Geoff was due to go to Spain the following day to try to sort out some work down there and seemed to be a bit nervous and on edge. He was drinking steadily and soon started to get at me about past articles from the newspapers. I know the only reason he feels jealous is because he cares about me, but given the amount I have to read about his alleged affairs, I do find it a bit annoying.

'Look,' I said, 'I'm really sick and tired of you going on about this, Geoff. If you can't forget the past then we've got to think seriously about having a little separation until you feel you can handle it. I want to live for today and for the future. We've got Jess to think about now and I just can't go on living like this with you raking over the past all the time.'

His response was to start accusing me of wanting to get rid of him and having someone else waiting in the wings to fill his shoes the moment he went away – as if I had the time let alone the inclination to be lining up men. He then stormed off from the table and when he returned he created a weird, tense atmosphere, speaking only in grunts and monosyllables. By now it was the end of the evening, so we said goodbye to everybody, got in a cab and drove home without speaking. I was cross that he had spoilt what should have been a nice evening before he went off to Spain again.

By the time we had finished saying goodnight to the babysitter and had gone upstairs it was after midnight and Jessie stirred in her cot as we went by. She often does that in the night and I usually give her a little pat on the back and settle her down again, but this time Geoff wanted to focus his attention on 'his little girl', so he picked her up and held her. I was quite happy for him to have a little diversion to help the atmosphere and Jess was delighted.

'I wanna go in your bed,' Jessie told him, so I had my wash and got into my nightdress while they cuddled on the bed. When I was ready to come to bed Jessie wanted to stay with Geoff, and since he seemed quite happy with the idea, and we weren't talking anyway, I tucked her in, said goodnight and went off to the single bed which we kept in her room.

As I settled down to sleep I could hear that she wasn't

settling and was chatting away to her dad. I assumed they were all right together and began to drift off. I was jerked back to wakefulness by the sound of footsteps marching across the bedroom and the next thing I knew I was being pulled out of bed. 'If you don't have any respect for yourself,' he snarled, 'at least have a bit of thought for your daughter when she's crying for you.' I was yanked out of the bed and thrown to the floor. It was all so quick I couldn't tell what had happened, but as I got up my nose was pumping out blood.

If Geoff had shown any signs of remorse or put his arm round my shoulders to comfort me everything would have been different, but he didn't and I felt really frightened and alone. He had never done anything like this before. There was blood all over my nightdress and the floor, and when I ran to the bathroom and leaned over the toilet it poured out like water out of a tap. There didn't seem to be any way to stop it flowing. I was pulling off handfuls of toilet tissue, but it was becoming soaked through within seconds.

'Look, Jessica,' Geoff was saying, cuddling her on his lap, 'look at silly Mummy. That's what happens when you're being silly and you fall over.' I could see that he was succeeding in keeping her calm, but he was doing nothing to allay my terror as the blood kept pouring out of me. Without thinking I ran downstairs to the telephone and called Mum. She answered immediately.

'Mum,' I cried, 'he's broken my nose.' I just needed someone to comfort and support me and she was the first person I thought of. I know I shouldn't do that sort of thing to her now that she's on her own, but I was desperate and I didn't stop to think. 'I don't know what to do.'

'All right, darling,' she said eventually, after expressing a few strong opinions about Geoff, 'I'm coming over.'

I could hear Geoff crashing down the stairs behind me and he snatched up the phone up as I put it down, dialling 999.

'What are you doing?' I wanted to know.

'I'm fed up with getting the blame for everything,' he shouted and it didn't seem to me that he knew what he was doing. 'Police, please,' he said into the phone, going on to tell them what had happened.

I couldn't believe he wanted to involve the police and I told him so. I said I thought he was just being stupid. As soon as the police arrived a few minutes later, I turned to go back upstairs with Jessica, telling them to go and that we were fine, and leaving Geoff to sort out his own mess. Jessie and I went into the bedroom and sat together on the bed. I could hear a commotion and angry voices downstairs, but I didn't want to show my face. There were footsteps on the stairs and I hugged Jessica tightly to me as a uniformed policeman appeared in the door.

'Are you all right?' he asked.

'Yes,' I nodded, rocking Jessica back and forth to comfort her.

'Do you want to press charges?'

'No, thank you.' I was adamant.

'What's your name?'

'Gillian Taylforth.' I watched as he wrote it down.

'What's your daughter's name?'

'Why do you want to know her name?' I felt myself panicking and becoming defensive.

'We have to say who was in the house at the time of the incident.'

'She's two and a half years old. You don't need to know her name.'

'Can I have your daughter's name, please?'

'No. I'm not going to tell you.'

'Look,' he said, 'I understand how you feel about us because of things that have happened in the past, but please don't tar us all with the same brush. We're not all from the same barrel.' I felt strangely lifted by these few kind words. To find a policeman who actually believed me made me feel chuffed even in the middle of such a dreadful scene.

I felt the tears starting and my voice cracked. 'Then you'll understand why I'm asking you to leave my house. I never called you, he did, please leave me alone.'

'Good night,' he said and went downstairs.

I went back into the bedroom and looked out the window. Outside I could see two policemen taking Geoff off in handcuffs, still barefooted and in his lemon dressing gown. I was so relieved when the house fell silent and they had all gone. I went back to cuddling Jessica.

When Mum and Debbie arrived they propped me up with cushions, because I couldn't breathe through my nose by then and I was frightened to blow it in case I started the bleeding off again. I dozed for a while. Later in the morning Geoff's mum, Jean, and his younger brother Roland came to pick up some of Geoff's stuff because he needed clothes to appear before the magistrates. He was still due to go down to Spain. Roland is like 'Mr Sensible' and is often the best one to calm Geoff down when he's angry. They told me he was out on unconditional bail and was waiting in a car down the road. The police had said he couldn't appear before the magistrates in prison clothes and should get some of his own stuff.

'What's he charged with?' I wanted to know.

'Assaulting a police officer.'

'Is he all right?'

'Not too good,' Roland said. 'His head's come up in a great lump where they hit him with a truncheon.'

The rest of the day went past me in a haze, but every arrival and departure of friends and family was religiously logged by the press pack who had arrived as soon as the news got out and did not go away. I rang the BBC to tell them what was happening, and they offered to send the doctor from the clinic they use at Borehamwood. The doctor looked at the state of my eyes and at the swelling on my nose, and advised me to have an X-ray to see if it was broken. He would arrange an appointment in a few days' time, when it had settled down a bit.

Outside we could see the press circling round his car like hyenas, peering in through the windows. 'I'm afraid they'll know I'm a doctor,' he said, 'from the stickers on the car.'

'It's okay,' I assured him.

As he got ready to go he said, 'Don't worry, I won't say a word,' and strode off to his car with a firm expression on his face.

The press stayed on in force. We had to pin a sheet up at the kitchen windows to stop them photographing us inside. One man on a motorbike followed me everywhere I went for a couple of days, which was unsettling. At least I assume he was from the press, but I suppose he could have been anyone, since they had printed my address in the papers for all to read. The neighbours, whom we have now got to know well, were wonderful. They kept watch on the street for us and pushed little notes through the letterbox whenever a new batch of reporters or photographers had been spotted hiding round a different corner, waiting for us. Some of them actually went up to the press and tried to make them go away. Eventually we all dashed out to cars and headed off to Mum's.

The next morning the front pages of the *Sun*, the *Daily Mirror* and the *Daily Star* were covered in headlines about the incident; inside pages gave every detail of the previous day, as well as rehashing everything from the cuttings files, including the A1 and the court case. They said that a policeman's face, ribs and back had been cut during a scuffle in the house when they came in answer to Geoff's call, and that one of the officers had fallen down the stairs during a struggle. The paper attributed all the information to anonymous 'neighbours', quoting them as saying that they were often woken up by our endless rows. Since then every one of the people who live around us has been in to tell us that they were horrified that we might think they would say any such thing and they had never heard us rowing. They needn't have worried, I never for a moment imagined they had. They have been a wonderful bunch of people and I have been very touched by the way they have stuck up for us and helped us when we have caused their quiet little cul-de-sac to come under repeated siege.

Once the story was out the Sunday papers became frantic to get more details during Saturday and tracked us to Mum's place. Ronnie came round to give us moral support. We decided to go to Kim's for the day for some peace and quiet and refused to comment on the way to the car. All day long a *News of the World* reporter kept phoning us. Ronnie took the calls and the man managed to convince him that they only wanted to tell the truth in order to help me. Ronnie wasn't feeling too kindly disposed towards Geoff at that moment and thought this reporter seemed all right. 'We would like you to talk to us, Ronnie,' the man said. 'We could offer you £30,000.' Ronnie laughed and suggested he would have to double the offer. 'I'll need to check back about that,' the man said.

Ronnie was gob-smacked: 'They're thinking of giving me £60,000 for an interview.' He told me what the man had said and I agreed that it did sound as if he was quite a nice bloke but there was still no way we were going to talk to them. When the man came back Ronnie asked him to leave us alone, and he promised to do so. That evening we headed back to Mum's place and saw the reporter's car still outside the front. Ronnie was furious and drove Mum, Aunt Shirley, Jessie and me round to the back entrance, which is past the rubbish chutes, and then took the car to the front with his baby, Chloe. Aunt Shirley went ahead to unlock the front door for us.

After parking the car Ronnie went over to the reporter. 'Hallo, mate,' he said, 'what are you still doing here?' As they talked another man got out of a car and started to walk round to the back of the flats. 'Who's that?' Ronnie asked.

'Oh,' the reporter stammered, 'he must be with us.'

Meanwhile, deciding the coast was clear, Mum and I had started to walk towards the car when we saw a guy coming round from the front.

'Quick, Gill, he's got a camera,' Mum shouted, and we ran up behind the chutes. I could hear the camera snapping away, getting shots of the back of my head. The photographer came back round to the front of the flats as I ran along the balcony towards the front door.

Ronnie had run back into the flats by now, and he shouted at Mum, 'Hold the baby,' thrusting Chloe towards her.

'No, Ronnie,' Mum tried to calm him.

'Hold the baby!' he shouted in a voice that made even Mum jump. She took Chloe from him, catching me up. Ronnie then grabbed hold of the photographer and pushed him against the bonnet of a parked car. 'If you take one more photograph of that girl,' he warned, 'I'll kill you.' I had never seen Ronnie that angry.

When the men had finally gone and we were back inside, Ronnie was still shaking. 'You know, Gilly,' he said, 'I've always thought of myself as a pretty streetwise person. I've always known when someone's not being straight with me, but with these people you just never know.'

'Ten years I've been doing this show now, Ron,' I said, 'and I still can't tell which ones are genuinely nice and which ones are pretending to be nice to stitch you up.'

The following day the stories bore almost no resemblance to anything which had been said or done by any of us and one paper actually had a letter from the girl who had accused Geoff of beating her up in Spain, advising me to dump him as she had. I went to the hospital that the doctor had recommended and once the swelling had gone down they were able to tell me that my nose was fractured, not broken, but that it was slightly crooked. It was something which they could easily fix in one afternoon.

The stories continued to appear during the week, as did the rings on the doorbell and telephone. I went into work for a bit and everyone was very nice, saying that I should take a few days off. Most of the press coverage was very sympathetic to me now – I had changed in the media's perception from the 'coarse, drunken actress with a sausage' to the 'battered victim of a violent man'. Everyone kept giving me advice – people who'd never met me but happened to write for newspapers; friends, relatives, colleagues – everyone had an opinion about what I should do. Most of the opinions centred on throwing Geoff out of the house and never having anything more to do with him. But he's Jessica's dad and she loves him, and whatever anyone else says, that was the first time he had ever laid a finger on me. I believe he shocked himself with what he did that night. I had been telling him for ages that he should do something about learning to control his temper and now he had proof that he had to do something if we were to have any chance of surviving together.

In the *Daily Mail* Lynda Lee Potter very kindly paid me

some compliments, saying I was 'very pretty, a good actress and a warm-hearted woman', but then rather spoilt it by asking why I stayed with Geoff and concluding that over the last five 'increasingly sad years the laughing, confident, merry-hearted girl has lost her confidence and her self-esteem. She's beginning to feel, as so many women trapped by violent men feel, that she's worthless, that nobody else would want her. She interprets his violence as proof that he really cares.' She described Geoff as 'thuggish, unfaithful and violent' and suggested that the basket of flowers which he sent me to say sorry was probably paid for with my money.

'She is living in a rented house,' she went on, 'she has to cope with ribald comments wherever she goes, look after her two-year-old daughter and work the relentless schedules involved in having a major part in a soap that now goes out three times a week. She remains loyal to Knights and continually explains away yet another clouting by transparently thin excuses.' I'm grateful for the kind words and support, but what's this 'yet another clouting'?

Her conclusion was that I was clinging to Geoff 'like a drowning woman might cling to a piece of rotten driftwood as it drags her out to sea – before finally disintegrating and leaving her to drown'. That's something to look forward to then.

Vanessa in the *Daily Mirror* kindly said that I was a 'powerfully gifted performer,' and then turned it into a backhanded compliment by adding, 'but dark glasses and her considerable acting skills don't even come close to masking her pain' and going on to suggest that perhaps I had agreed to give Geoff oral sex in the Range Rover because I was 'too scared of the consequences to refuse'.

Today had the idea of writing me an 'open letter' from Barbara Windsor, headlined 'A word in your shell-like, Gillian

– How one EastEnder who has had her troubles might advise another who attracts disaster like a magnet.'

One of the stories said that a new edition of Trivial Pursuit had been produced with half a dozen questions about me, the A1 and Range Rovers in it. On one occasion quite soon after I heard about this I found I was alone in the house. I went upstairs to the bedroom and just started to sob, unable to stop myself. I had thought there was nothing else they could do to hurt me, but now I really thought that Jessica might be better off in life without me. I could just imagine her as a teenager going to a party with some of her friends, someone getting out Trivial Pursuit and starting to play. I could picture how embarrassed she would be when her mother's name came up in a question about oral sex. If it hadn't been for my determination not to give up, for Jessica's sake, the prospect might have seemed too awful to bear.

21

A New Year and a New Start

I've never been one to wish my life away, but I was so glad to see the end of 1994 – even though it meant all the magazines and television channels were full of 'round-ups' of the year's events, which inevitably included references to sausages and court cases. I feel, however, that I am finally becoming able to handle the jokes and the jibes. I realise that the publication of this book will bring it all back to people's attention again, which is a bit daunting, but I think it's worth putting up with if it gives me an opportunity to tell my story the way it was.

One morning Mum rang and said, 'I see the papers say you and Ross are having an affair now.' (Ross Kemp is the actor who plays Grant Mitchell in *EastEnders*.)

'They what?' I exploded down the line. 'How could they possibly say that? I've had just about enough of this, it's bloody ridiculous. His girlfriend is really going to love that, isn't she?'

'No, in the series, Gillian.' Mum realised I had got the wrong end of the stick. 'They think Kathy and Grant are going to have an affair.'

That put it all in perspective for me, really. The whole thing had become one enormous soap opera and as long as I could put up with the odd comment in the street I could miss most of the rubbish by not reading the papers any more. As long as I want to keep acting people are going to remember the stories of 1994 and I realise now that I'm just going to have to accept it.

One of the things which helped to get me through the year was my work. I love my job so much and it is so demanding that it doesn't leave me much time to think and brood over things. It's impossible to do that sort of work if you are moping and feeling sorry for yourself. You have to learn the lines and do the scenes to the best of your ability and that absorbs all your energy, taking you out of yourself. I dread to think how depressed I would have become if I had given that up and gone into hiding, but between the series and looking after Jessie I've been kept busy. It's been tiring, but I think it has been what has got me through.

Now that Jessie is nearly three and becoming more independent – not to mention bossy – every day, I'm beginning to think that it might be nice to give her a brother or sister. It would be lovely to have another little person around who really needed me and no one else. I've even been catching myself going through the cast lists in the *Radio Times* – pages and pages of them! – looking at all the names and deciding which ones I think would be nice for a baby . . . It was just the same back in 1991: months before I actually fell pregnant I'd find myself spending more time reading the credits than I did watching the programmes! So I reckon it's a sure sign that I'm getting broody again.

At work I spend a lot of time with the the twins who play Kathy's grandchildren, plus Adam's little Jessica, who gets brought in sometimes. They're so lovely. And several of my other friends are pregnant, which brings back all the happy memories. Since I'm approaching forty now I've got to make any decisions in that area pretty quickly.

Geoff and I also saw the new year as an opportunity for a new start for us. With all the pressures that were put upon us by the media and money worries, it was not surprising that our relationship nearly went on the rocks. But we want to be together and to give Jessie a stable home life, and if we do ever part we want it to be because we have decided it's not working, not because everyone else is telling us to call it a day.

A lot of my friends are going to be leaving *EastEnders* in 1995, including Bill (Arthur), Sue (Michelle), Letitia (Sharon), Lucy (Natalie) and Nicola (Debbie). It will change things for all of us and although I feel very sad because I have been working with Bill, Sue and Tish since the first day the series went out ten years ago and have become very friendly with the other two in recent years, it is also exciting to think how the plots will develop to accommodate these changes. Of all the people who started the series, only Adam (Ian), Wendy (Pauline) and I will be left now. It's been a very exciting ten years, with far more ups than downs, and I can't wait to see what will happen next.

22

So, That's What Happened Next!

That was how I finished the first edition of the book back at the end of 1994, all optimistic and expecting things to settle themselves down so that we could get on with a quiet life. No such luck! What I should have been saying was, 'Fasten your seats belts, 1995 is about to be a very bumpy ride indeed.'

Three weeks after the beginning of the new year I went in to work as usual on a Monday. Lunchtime came round and someone asked if I was going up to have a drink with one of the writers, who was celebrating his hundredth edition of the show or some such milestone.

'Oh yeah,' I said cheerfully, 'that would be nice,' and I went up to have a couple of glasses of wine. I hadn't eaten anything since lunchtime the day before because we had got home too late for supper and breakfast had been the usual rush.

About three o'clock I went on set and did my scenes. Back in my dressing room, doing some mail, I was asked down to costume for somebody's leaving do. I went along and had a glass of wine with them before going to the crèche to pick up Jessie and have a bit of a chat with the girls who look after her. I then drove out of the studios.

I had just bought a new BMW and I was still not quite sure how to operate the straps holding Jessie in her new seat. As I turned the first corner she dropped her dummy on the floor and wriggled herself under the belt to try to retrieve it.

'Leave it, darling,' I said, turning my head. 'Mummy'll get it when she stops.' As I turned back I moved the steering wheel too abruptly, unused to the power steering, and went straight into the back of a parked car.

I doubt if I was doing more than twenty miles an hour and there was little more than a loud 'thud' which made Jessie look up in surprise and say, 'Mummy.' Once I had seen that she was all right I relaxed into a complete flap. I tried to reverse the car into a better position and found myself going up on to the pavement and scraping someone's garden wall. I realised that I was now in no fit state to do anything and got out, shaking like a leaf. By this time a small group of people had gathered round and the full horror of what might have happened if I'd been going any faster hit me. As I lifted Jessie out of the car she realised I was crying and that started her off. Several people recognised me and someone advised me to turn the engine off.

Some people came out of the house behind the wall which I had hit and told me it was also their car I had run into. 'I'm really sorry,' was all I could think to say.

They couldn't have been nicer about the whole thing. They realised how shaken up I was and invited me in to sit down. Their children came to play with Jessie and we had a cup of tea. 'Do you mind if I phone my boyfriend?' I asked and they showed me where the phone was.

I called Geoff and told him I had had a crash. He went mad. 'Have you been drinking?' he wanted to know.

'Well,' I thought back, 'I did have a couple of glasses of wine at lunchtime, but that's all.' For the first time it occurred to me that perhaps I might be slightly over the limit.

Quarter of an hour later Geoff turned up at the house. He strode in, took one look at me, scooped Jessie up, said, 'Don't bother coming home' and went off with her.

I thought, 'Thanks for your support.' Perhaps I would have reacted the same way if it had been him who had endangered Jessica's life, but I could have done with a little more sympathy than that. I was left sitting in these people's front room, wondering what to do next.

The decision was taken out of my hands when the police turned up.

'Oh hallo, Kath,' one of them said as he came into the room. 'Third time lucky, eh?'

'What are you doing here?' I asked. 'I haven't killed anybody or anything.'

'No,' he snapped back, 'but you could've done!'

This didn't seem the most tactful thing to say, since my mind had been full of nothing but images of what might have happened, most of them involving Jessie flying through the windscreen. I was feeling shaken and mortified enough by what I had done. I kept asking myself, 'Why didn't you get a cab home?' but the answer was always the same, 'Because I thought I was all right.'

'Could you blow into this for us.' The officer held up a breathalyser. I took it from him, but I was shaking so much I couldn't get my breath. It felt as if I was having a panic attack of some sort.

'You'll have to excuse me,' I puffed, 'I get this nervous asthma thing.'

'Blow into it,' he said impatiently. 'Just do it, now.'

I put it to my lips and tried to blow, but I couldn't get enough air into my lungs to do it. I took it out of my mouth to try again. 'Are we going to be all day about this?' he demanded angrily.

Eventually I managed to get my breath and he glanced at the results. 'Right,' he said, 'you're over. You'll have to come down to the station with us.' He read me my rights and for a moment I thought he was going to handcuff me. I started to cry again as he led me out to the car.

'I just want you to know,' the lady of the house said as I went past, 'it wasn't us that called them.'

'Don't worry,' I assured her, 'they would have turned up if I'd driven over a matchstick.'

While they took all my details at the police station, I phoned my sister Janice and asked her to come down and get me. They tested me again and I was still over, so it was time to line up in front of the camera, holding a number up in front of me, just like in all the crime movies you've ever seen. The photographer kept trying to get me to put my head up, but I couldn't stop crying.

'You'll probably have some press outside,' they told us as we got ready to leave. 'We had to phone to let them know you were here.'

'What do you mean,' Janice demanded, 'you *had* to phone?'

Janice took me back to her house and we heard that the press were waiting for me to get back home to Whetstone. The next morning the papers were full of the story. They said the car was a write-off (which it wasn't, because the garage had it fixed three days later) and they had taken pictures from angles which made it look like a mangled mess. The worst thing, however, was that they now decided I had a serious drink problem. Apparently, every lunchtime at work I have to have a bottle of champagne in my dressing room and every half-hour the directors have to let me off set so that I can go back for a swift one. Geoff was quoted as saying a few things about my abilities as a mother, which made my mum so angry she refused to speak to him. By the weekend the papers were reporting that I was checking into a drink clinic. Someone asked me if I was going to sue and I thought, 'Oh, please! Lose another couple of hundred grand?'

The case came up in February and I went before the magistrate armed with letters from my doctor and psychiatrist explaining that I was suffering from post-traumatic stress. I was given a twenty-three-month ban and fined about five hundred quid. They told me they were being lenient because I had had twenty years with no driving offences at all. I thought twenty-three months was a bit steep, but I could understand why they felt they needed to make an example of me. One friend told me afterwards they had thought I might be put away for three months, which I think would have been very, very steep – but would have made this a very exciting chapter! Being without a car has certainly been a salutary lesson to me.

My next problem was working out the best way to get to and from work and other places, which basically came down to taxis. I rang a local cab company and they suggested I had a regular driver and paid at the end of the week rather than rustling up the fare every time I wanted to go anywhere. I had the same driver most of the time and we became good friends in the course of our daily routines. He had a little girl who was about the same age as Jessie.

Things were a bit tense between Geoff and me – I was sick and tired of the arguments and rows and I decided I wanted to have more time to myself. I said I wanted to rent a place of my own to get a better perspective on things. Geoff didn't like the idea, but he could see that I was serious. I had a list of properties and the driver took me round to see them on my days off. Geoff wasn't too happy about me spending so much time with another man either, but since he didn't have time to drive me himself there wasn't much either of us could do about that.

I was still looking around when Easter came along. Geoff and I went to a party at a friend's house on the Saturday and had a really nice time. On the Sunday we went round to Geoff's sister's house. Geoff had been drinking before we got there and on the way he started in on me about my family's attitude towards him. By the time we arrived there was an atmosphere between us which everyone could sense. At one stage I sat down on the stairs with Geoff's brother Steve and he asked me how things were going. I tried to explain why my family were so cross with Geoff. I didn't realise that Geoff was leaning over the banisters upstairs, listening, until he came storming down and pushed his way past other guests, out of the front door and off to the pub.

Geoff's niece took me home that evening and after putting Jessie to bed I started to think; I really didn't want to be around when Geoff got back from the pub. I decided to take Jessie and spend the night at a hotel up the road. When he had calmed down the next day we would be able to talk. I called my driver at about eleven o'clock and asked if he would come and pick us up. Jessie was asleep by then, so when I heard the car I lifted her without waking her and carried her downstairs. The driver took Jessie's bag out to the car and then came back.

'Here,' I passed Jessie over to him, 'can you take her while I get my bag?'

At that moment Geoff turned up and events became a terrible blur. All I remember is the two of them rolling around on the grass, shouting and punching. There was a lot of blood. For some reason I thought I might be able to separate them, which was stupid; I just got kicked and punched in the mêlée, reeling back from a blow to the head.

Hysterical by then, I ran back into the house and phoned the police. They arrived a few minutes later and broke the fight up. The driver looked a terrible mess and the police called an ambulance for him. I remember crying and shouting at Geoff, 'You idiot! You idiot! You always get it wrong!' And then I passed out.

By the next morning, after a visit to the hospital to check the lump on my head, and then a few hours' sleep at the hotel with Jessie safely at my sister Debbie's, I began to feel really annoyed at Geoff for creating yet another stupid incident. The police asked if I wanted to press charges. Initially I said no, but they talked to me a bit more and pointed out that I was willing to speak up for the driver, so why didn't I think I was worthy of some protection? In the heat of the moment I agreed.

A couple of weeks later I regretted that decision bitterly, realising that if I was to testify against Geoff and he was put in prison I would one day have to explain to Jessie that I had helped to put her father away. I just couldn't do that. I also found the prospect of going back into court, even as a witness, too horrible to contemplate. My psychiatrist said he thought it would be bad for me, not to mention the fact that I knew anything I said in court would mean more coverage in the papers, as well as having to take time off work. I went back to the police and told them that now I had had time to think about it I didn't want to press charges.

The media, needless to say, came out with a hundred different articles and interviews about the incident, branding Geoff as 'Beastender' and God knows what else. One newspaper had meanwhile managed to find some skeletons in the driver's past about him being an ex-copper and having been inside for fraud. The whole thing became very ugly and I was back to not being able to leave the house without reporters and photographers leaping out of cars and firing questions at me. However I had seen an advertisement for a beautician's called Jill's in Potters Bar that offered CACI non-surgical face-lifts. I decided to give myself a treat and went along. It made me feel really good, so I have been going ever since and Jill and I have become great friends.

Geoff had been banned from seeing me because I was now a prosecution witness. He went to live with his brother Steve and could only see Jessie if someone else picked her up and took her to him. To start with the separation was a relief to me, giving me the time away from him which I had been saying I needed. At that stage I hoped that I would never see him again. After a month apart, however, I realised that I was starting to miss him. I used to feel so sad when Pete or Jean picked Jessie up and took her off to see her dad – it was exactly the sort of life I didn't want for my family. But I was able to hear how Geoff was getting on by seeing his mum and dad or Roland.

In July the contract ran out on the house in Whetstone and Geoff sent a message suggesting that as his house in Nazeing was empty, Jessie and I should move in there until we found somewhere we liked. It seemed an ideal arrangement, but it meant the press were back outside the door. At one stage they even mistook Roland for his brother and accused me of seeing Geoff on the quiet, threatening to tell the police if we didn't come out of the house and talk to them.

On the whole, however, life settled down into a reasonable routine and I found I had a lot more time for friends and family if I didn't have to worry about my relationship with Geoff all the time. Then one day in August I had Jessie in the crèche at work when I discovered I was going to be finishing late. I phoned a few people to find someone to pick Jess up, but no one was in. I called Geoff's work and left a message with his partner, who said he would get him to do it. It was a Wednesday night and they were recording *Top of the Pops*, so there was a big crowd outside the studio as I took Jess down to the gates during one of my breaks. I could see Geoff parked on the opposite side of the road, but there was no one I could ask to take Jess across. As I came out of the gates a couple of lads, drinking from beer cans, started shouting at me about blow jobs, which angered and flustered me. Not wanting to answer them back in front of Jess, I kept my eyes on the ground and walked on. I didn't want to come back past these lads, so when I got to the car I asked Geoff just to run me to the top of the road so that I could wait for them to go before coming back in. He dropped me at the shops and went off with Jessie. By the time I got back to the studio the crowd had disappeared and I was able to go back to work.

That Sunday the *Sunday Mirror* had the banner headline 'Jailbait', with pictures of me getting into the car with Geoff. The police arrested Geoff the following week and locked him up in Wormwood Scrubs for the weekend. I guess the photographers must have been following us all those months, just waiting for the chance to catch us out.

I was very frightened about going back to court in case they didn't believe me again and I ended up being done for perjury. I had a very tight filming schedule and had to appear in the dock between doing two quite hard scenes, so I was not in the calmest of moods. The magistrate was very patronising. 'Well, Miss Taylforth,' she proclaimed grandly, 'you may be an actress by profession, but this is the real world now!' Not a very objective start to the proceedings, I thought. 'I also hear,' she continued, 'that you have been giving interviews to the press,' which I most certainly had not. She listened to what I had to say and said, 'Umm, well, I suppose we'll have to take your word for it.'

Now all we had to get through was Geoff's trial over the incident with the driver. We had more or less prepared ourselves for the fact that this time he would probably go away for a few years. I hated the idea of Jessie's father being taken away from her like that and I dreaded the day.

The case was due to be heard on 16 October, but Geoff's barrister felt that the case had been prejudiced by the adverse publicity Geoff had received during the lead-up to the trial. To give the barrister time to research, another date was set for Friday 29 September, when the arguments would be heard. At this meeting both the prosecution and the defence agreed that there was a strong case for dismissal of the charges, although the prosecution still fought for the case to proceed. The judge decided that he required the weekend to analyse all the evidence and would then make his decision. On the Monday I was in work when someone told me to go to make-up because one of the girls wanted to talk to me. I went in and found Geoff sitting there.

'It's been thrown out,' he told me, grinning with relief.

We had made history. That night Geoff's picture was up behind the newscasters on the main bulletins and questions were being raised as to whether all the tabloid newspaper editors were guilty of contempt of court for making it impossible for Geoff to stand trial. An inquiry was to be set up and the papers were sent to the Attorney-General, Sir Nicholas Lyell. He decided that the editors of the papers were not guilty of any wrong-doing, which has left a rather confused picture of the whole business.

So we ended another traumatic year, hoping that things would finally calm down and improve. So far in 1996 we do seem to be getting somewhere. Writing this book gave me a chance to sort out some of my debts with the *Sun* and I have bought a lovely new house for us to start afresh. In April I was asked to be a guest host on the *Big Breakfast* and it went really well, boosting my confidence and making me feel that I did the right thing to keep working throughout all the troubles, giving myself something to hang on to and build from.

At work, Kathy has had her baby, Ben, who has made absolutely everyone on the programme come over broody, and there was a big publicity campaign with pictures of us by Lord Lichfield on the cover of *Radio Times* and virtually every other TV magazine. Having had some pictures taken by Snowdon during the publicity campaign for the book I've actually been getting some portraits of myself that I quite like for once.

Bill, Sue and 'Tish have all left *EastEnders* now, and I really miss all of them. Bill is such a great character, and he used to make me laugh so much with his mucking about. I socialised with Sue and 'Tish a lot over the years, and you do tend to lose touch once people move on from the series. On a daily basis it doesn't feel as though that much has changed, because we're always working on different scenes in different studios, so sometimes you don't see other members of the cast for weeks at a time anyway. But in fact Wendy, Adam and I are now the only original members of the cast left. Adam was having a look at the production computer recently and discovered that I am approaching my thousandth episode, having done more than anybody else, even him and Wendy.

Barbara Windsor and I get on very well. We've realised that we are both Leos and our lives seem to have so many similarities. And the Albert Square plot-lines keep coming thick and fast; at the time of writing Ian has just been shot and nobody knows whether Tiffany is going to have her baby or not . . .

Of course, the blow-job jokes haven't gone away completely. There are still young men in passing cars or on street corners who shout and make gestures, even if Jessica is watching them, but they are gradually getting fewer. When Geoff had another attack of pancreatitis in February, and it even looked as if we might lose him, the *Sun* couldn't resist an editorial comment about me rushing to his bedside with my special cure – 'which you can't get on the NHS'. I couldn't believe that they could print something like that before he was out of danger.

So, here we are again, bruised but optimistic. I feel I am so much stronger than I was when I first started writing this story a couple of years ago. It has been a great help to be able to let people know a bit about what has really been happening behind all the hysterical headlines and hype. I hope now that we can *really* settle down and get on with the sort of family life I want for Jessie.